THE POWER *of* GRIT
in the Classroom, School and Community

Developing Perseverance, a Passion to Meet Short-term and Long-term Goals, Building a Positive Gritty School and Community Culture, Impacting Social & Emotional Learning and Growth Mindset in Your Students and School.

Heavenly Realm Publishing
Houston, Texas

STEPHANIE FRANKLIN

This book is protected by the copyright laws of the United States. This book may not be copied or reprinted for commercial gain or profit. No part of this book may be reproduced, stored in a retrieval system, or transmitted by any means, electronic, mechanical, photocopying, recording, or otherwise, without written permission from the author and publisher.

Copyright © 2021 by, Stephanie Franklin, The Power of Grit in the Classroom, School and Community: *Developing Perseverance, a Passion to Meet Short-term and Long-term Goals, Building a Positive Gritty School and Community Culture, Impacting Social & Emotional Learning and Growth Mindset in Your Students and School. All rights reserved.*

Published by,
Heavenly Realm Publishing
www.heavenlyrealmpublishing.com
1-866-216-0696

Visit our website at: www.heavenlyrealmpublishing.com

Printed in the United States of America

ISBN—13- 9781944383282 (paperback)
ISBN—13- 9781944383299 (hardback)

Library of Congress Registration: 2021915806

1. EDUCATION / Educational Psychology: The Power of Grit in the Classroom, School and Community: *Developing Perseverance, a Passion to Meet Short-term and Long-term Goals, Building a Positive Gritty School and Community Culture, Impacting Social & Emotional Learning and Growth Mindset in Your Students and School. /* Stephanie Franklin. / **2. EDUCATION / General:** The Power of Grit in the Classroom, School and Community: *Developing Perseverance, a Passion to Meet Short-term and Long-term Goals, Building a Positive Gritty School and Community Culture, Impacting Social & Emotional Learning and Growth Mindset in Your Students and School. /* Stephanie Franklin. / **3. PSYCHOLOGY / Cognitive Psychology & Cognition:** The Power of Grit in the Classroom, School and Community: *Developing Perseverance, a Passion to Meet Short-term and Long-term Goals, Building a Positive Gritty School and Community Culture, Impacting Social & Emotional Learning and Growth Mindset in Your Students and School. /* Stephanie Franklin.

This book is printed on acid free paper.

THE POWER *of* GRIT
in the Classroom, School and Community

Gritty Sayings by Prominent People

Grit is the grain that builds character.
— ***Edwin Percy Whipple***

Grit is the persistence in following your own destiny.
—***Paul Bradley Smith***

Grit is having the courage to do the right thing, regardless of the popularity or consequences.
— ***Joan Hall***

What is grit? Grit is refusing to give up. It's persistence.
—***Peter H. Diamandis***

"Grit is not just simple elbow-grease term for rugged persistence. It is an often-invisible display of endurance that lets you stay in an uncomfortable place, work hard to improve upon a given interest and do it again and again."
—***Sarah Lewis***

Grit is the piece to the puzzle for students who exemplify a passion and perseverance to learn against all odds, and for teachers and administrators who attains a passion and perseverance to teach in a gritty way to help students to be successful in their life-long learning.
—***Stephanie Franklin***

*For my mother and father who passed while I completed this project,
may you both rest in peace.*

*For every gritty student, teacher, principal, staff, stakeholder,
parent and community leader who is striving to
gain success whether in your classroom,
school, home, business, or community.*

—Stephanie Franklin

Rita Pierson, a teacher for 40 years, once heard a colleague say, "They don't pay me to like the kids." Her response: "Kids don't learn from people they don't like." A rousing call to educators to believe in their students and actually connect with them on a real, human, personal level.

"Let's get in good trouble, necessary trouble…"

—John Lewis

"We must ensure that <u>all</u> students have the proper education, and teachers, administrators and staff have <u>all</u> the opportunities they deserve."

—Stephanie Franklin

For Leaders--Teachers & Staff

It is important for teachers and staff to work together on the common goal of preparing our youth for their future. If teachers and staff do not place a value on academics, technology or grit in the classroom, an integral piece of the puzzle is missing. A link between the two entities will
create a deeper level of collaboration and cooperation
as they two work cohesively together.
—*Stephanie Franklin*

For Leaders—Principals & Administrators

It is important for principals and administrators to work together on the common goal of preparing our youth for their future. If principals and administrators do not place a value on academics, technology or grit in the classroom and school, an integral piece of the puzzle is missing. A link between the two entities will create a deeper level of collaboration and cooperation as they two work cohesively together.

—*Stephanie Franklin*

*For you "Momma," I finally finished the book.
Wish you were here to celebrate.
Thank you for believing in me. I miss you very much!* ♡

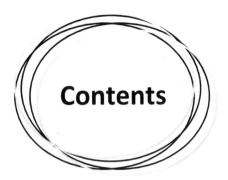

Contents

Introduction.......... 15

Chapters:

1. What Does it Mean to Have Grit?.......... 29
2. Developing the Power of Grit in Your Students and in Your School.......... 39
3. Why is Grit Important for Your Students? 45
4. How Do You Teach Grit? 49
5. What is Grit and Growth Mindset? 59
6. Building a Positive School Culture and Climate Through Grit and Growth Mindset.......... 73
7. Grit—A Two-Edged Sword: *How It Applies to At-Risk Students & SEL (Social Emotional Learning) Students*.......... 79
8. True Grit: *The Best Measure of Success and How to Teach It*.......... 85
9. What is An Example of Grit? 89
10. Is Grit Really the Key to Success? 91
11. What Are the Five Characteristics of Grit? *How Many Can You List?* 97
12. Embrace Social & Emotional Learning with Grit 99
    - *Why is Social Emotional Learning Needed in the School District?*
    - *Using Social & Emotional Learning with Grit*
    - *How to Use Grit in mentorship and Social Emotional Learning*
    - *Controlling Your Actions*
    - *Success Comes with The Best*
    - *Build a Culture of Collaboration*
    - *Why Practice Self-Awareness in the Classroom?*

Contents

13. How Grit Applies to RTI (Response to Intervention).....117
14. How TTESS *(Texas Teacher Evaluation & Support System)* Applies to Grit 125
15. The Grit Characteristic Check: *How Many Do You Have?* 129
16. How Can I Help My Child Develop Grit? 135
17. How Do You Raise a Gritty Child? 141
18. What Does Grit Stand for in Our Schools? 147
19. What Does Grit Stand for in Your Community? 149
20. How Do I Make a Difference in My Community Using Grit? 157
21. Should Grit Be Taught in School? 161
22. Is Grit a Character Trait? 177
* Professional Developments 187
* Gritty Goals: *For the Teacher* 229
* Gritty Goals: *For the Principal* 233
* *Why is Corporative Learning Important to Setting Gritty Goals?* 236
* *The Jigsaw Classroom Cooperative Learning Technique* 237
* Checklist: Cooperative Learning 242
    1. Success Factors
    2. Turn-To-Your-Neighbor
    3. Think, Pair, Share
    4. Jigsaw
    5. Value Line
    6. Round Table
* Synthesis & Take Action 245
* Self-Awareness Activities 258
* Curriculum & Instruction: *How Does Curriculum & Instruction Fit into Culture, Leadership, and Learning on Your Campus or Classroom?* 268

- Instructional Gritty Play Action Book for Your School and/or Classroom 271
- Strategies for Learner-Friendly Environment Survey......... 283
- THE GRIT BUCKET LIST: *Barriers to Educational Opportunity That Challenges Gritty Achievement*.......... 285
- Index 293
- Chapter 22, Is Grit a Character Trait? Professional Development 3 Answer KEY 298
- *Meet the Author 300*

Know the power of the passion to succeed that lies within you and persevere to the end until you reach your goal.

—Stephanie Franklin

Introduction

When I was in grad school, I heard the most outstanding speech I had ever heard from an inspirational story: "An Empty Pickle Jar" from the book: "Stress Is a Choice," by Dave Zerfoss, (2011) who spoke to his philosophy class. He took a gallon glass clear empty pickle jar and filled it with golf balls and asked, "Is it full?" The class all agreed.

He then slowly poured a box of pebbles inside of the jar and lightly shook it, as the pebbles rolled down through the open areas of the golf balls on to the bottom and rose to the top. He then asked the students, "is it full now?" They all agreed.

The professor then picked up a box of sand and poured it in the jar covering everything as it filled on up to the top. He asked again, "Is it full yet?" All of the students responded, "yes."

The word "grit" impacts and fosters learning as it is a means to have passion and exemplify perseverance to endure through any challenge that may come your way...

The professor then took two glasses of chocolate milk from underneath the table and completely filled the jar as it covered the empty spaces between the sand.

His students laughed, looked on and were inspired by his teaching and by his credentials as he explained the moral of the story, "...This jar represents your life. The golf balls are the important

Introduction

things…your family, your children, your health, your friends, your favorite passions. Things that if everything else was lost and only they remained, your life would still be full."

"The pebbles are the other things that matter like your job, your home, your car."

"The sand is everything else…The small stuff. If you put the sand into the jar first, there is no room for the pebbles or the golf balls. The same goes for life. If you spend all your time and energy on the small stuff, you will never have room for the things that are critical to your happiness."

"Play with your children. Take time to get medical checkups. Take your partner to dinner. Play another 18. There will always be time to clean the house or fix the disposal."

"Take care of the golf balls first, the things that really matter. Set your priorities, the rest is just sand."

It is important to focus on the important things in life as you practice grit in all these areas—school, work, family and friends, making a difference in whatever compacity you choose, relationships, and in what you're passionate about every day. You must persevere when things get hard until you accomplish your goals. So, I ask you this question, is your jar half full or is it full?"

You as a teacher, staff, counselor, coach, assistant administrator or building principal should take a moment to enjoy yourself, your family, and your life. There will always be room for work. Zerfoss, (2011) is correct, "everyday is a gift." You should not take your life for granted. Teaching, leading and just working in the school district is not an easy career. However, it is the most rewarding career when you see the difference you make every day in the lives of students who need you in order to become successful in their academics, careers and in life.

Please take a moment to study what David Zerfoss, (2011) said and apply it to your own life and career. David spoke in a gritty way as to encourage every student, teacher, individual, assistant principal, principal, superintendent, and every district staff worker to persevere through all obstacles, even when the going gets tough, but mainly enjoy yourself and enjoy your life and not worry about the small stuff.

I wrote *The Power of Grit in the Classroom, School and Community* in hopes to show students, teachers, administrators, coaches, parents, the community and stakeholders how grit applies to their lives, education, and passion to succeed with perseverance and resilience to reach their goals.

I want teachers, principals, and staff to understand how grit plays a big part in their educational leadership within their school and classroom. I want parents to learn how to teach their children and youth, how to use grit in their homes and lives that foster hands-on-tools that inspire good character, kindness, self-growth, passion, purpose and perseverance.

Growing up in an urban side of town and having experienced the inner-city life that made me who I am today, I want to show my students and mentees how much I care about their life's purpose, education, academics, and social and emotional learning success because I understand struggle. I want teachers, staff, and principals to know that hard work does pay off through grit—true passion and perseverance and through making a difference in the lives of our students and school's educational accountability. I came across the most powerful word there is in the dictionary, "grit" that is so often hid.

The word "grit" impacts and fosters learning as it is a means to have passion and exemplify perseverance to endure through any challenge that may come your way whether it is educational, relational, social and emotional, family issues, unsuccessful friendships, athletic injuries, sports team brawls, within a school organization, or through business obstacles and challenges.

You may be a student, teacher, principal, assistant principal, superintendent, school staff, cafeteria cook, janitor, district

Introduction

maintenance worker, district administration, school board member, the PTO (Parent Teacher Association), business owner, co-worker, non-profit executive director, parent, those that work in some compacity of the school system, or just an individual that is trying to make it in life; and is doing whatever it takes to be successful, this book applies to you. Grit is a person with true grit—passion and perseverance who sets goals and commitments and follows through to complete them.

In today's diverse and inclusive schools and classrooms, it at times seems impossible to meet the needs of every student who walks through the doors, especially during the uncertainties of a pandemic. If you are a principal you may ask, "how do I reach and meet the needs of my school and staff throughout the year?" You as a teacher may ask, "how do I reach and meet the needs of my students throughout the year? How do I reach students who I teach virtually?" You as a student may ask, "how do I reach all of my teacher's expectations in order to be successful in all of their classes?" You as a parent may ask, "How do I reach and motivate my child to love learning at school?" You as a principal or teacher may also ask, "how do I help all the students excel? How do I know they are learning? How do I obtain a successful campus? How do I keep up with the latest to let my students know that I am not so deep that I cannot relate to them and what they are going through? How do I reach a Tier 1, Title 1 school with at-risk students?" All these questions are important factors that are being asked in every classroom and school leaving most principals, teachers and coaches questioning.

Grit is the key factor that helps the student, teacher, coach, principal, parent, community and stakeholder to persevere through every problem they may face while working hard to reach their goals. Grit allows you to understand how to be successful in reaching every student and meeting their academic and educational needs in a passionate and persevering way. So, how do you know you are gritty? Here is how you know: When you are leading as a first-year principal and leaving your first successful faculty meeting with a little encouragement that the teachers and staff seem to like you, within the next hour seeing a huge fight down the hallway and you're the only one to break it up. Perseverance. When teachers are constantly complaining about the same ol' thing with lack of motivation to collaborate to help make things better. Perseverance. When students come to your class and say, "this class sucks, I hate coming in here." Perseverance. You as the superintendent of schools visit a school and the faculty doesn't know who you are and lack any desire to make their campus and the students better. Perseverance and the passion for what you do has to ring in your ear drums constantly to remind you to stay passionate about what you do every day in spite of.

Each classroom should bring a diverse and cultural atmosphere each year. It is important to have classroom management, social-emotional learning, trauma-informed instruction, culturally response instruction, global perspectives and competencies, bullying and harassment interventions, and character-building education within your lessons. Teachers also need diversification within the workforce. There is a bridge and a wide gap between our students and teachers in these areas, especially with our minority students. Despite the effort of attending professional developments and trainings each year to become better in these areas, these gaps still exist. The problem is cyclical and needs special attention. Plain and simple, we need more grit and diversity in our schools and in front of the classroom as role models so that our students, especially minority students who may have less than other well-taken care of students can value school principals, teachers and teaching as a means to a career one day, or gritty confidence in finding their own path in whatever career they so choose.

Teachers play an essential role in the success of their students each school day and year. It is important to build a cultural climate for inquiry and understanding. There are eleven points I found

Introduction

important to name as you can use that will build a successful gritty school and classroom for the success of all students.

Students learn on:

1. Learner-centered pedagogies that are visually seen on the walls of your classroom, lab, and school.
2. Learner-centered banners posted up on the outside walls (outside of class and hallways) and curbsides of your classroom and school (bus ramp included).
3. Competency-based instruction and learning within your department and class lesson plans.
4. Teacher gritty leadership. Showing passion for all your students and not just the ones you feel comfortable with, or the ones that have all A's. Persevering when it seems as if your students are not learning to the compacity you think they should in your class.
5. Sharing your background and how you persevered through some rough times and how you made it through them. I do this all the time with my students and mentees in my class and mentoring program. I have found that it is okay to be candid and transparent about who you are by means to allow your students to not feel that you are way too deep, and too perfect to understand them and what they may be going through.
6. You are building instructional cultural and caring relationships (student to student, teacher to teacher, teacher to student, teacher to department chair, teacher to principal, teacher to assistant principal, assistant principal to assistant principal, assistant principal to principal, assistant principal to department, department chair and/or skills specialist to department, principal to staff, and principal to leadership team). Students watch everything you do, believe it or not. They know when you care and when you do not. They know when you do not like another teacher or principal.

They also know when you do not like them or another student. It is important to always exemplify positive professional leadership in front of your students even when you may be troubled with other co-workers, administration or students. Teaching students how to build innocent worthy relationships with one another builds not only culture, however, it allows them to understand one another and embrace who they are and their pasts.

7. You are getting gifted and talented and SPED (Special Education) students involved and allow them to be themselves and not feel left out, uncomfortable or afraid.
8. ELL- (English Language Learner), ESL- (English as a Second Language), ELA- (English Language Arts), TESOL- (Teaching English to Speakers of Other Languages). Selecting strategic activities that gear toward these areas for student understanding and learning.
9. RTI (Response to Interventions) in the school and classroom. Using this approach is very useful as it brings an academic approach to intervention that is needed in every school and classroom. Educator's RTI method helps students who are struggling with a skill, a lesson or a student who is at-risk for underperforming to appropriate grade level interventions. It is used to help each student to succeed in the classroom, and not just for children with special needs or learning disabilities, but for all students. It is also a multi-tier approach to early identification and support of students with learning and behavior needs. My mentor program that I lead has these types of students every day. I use RTI mentoring interventions and teaching procedures that help toward their negative behavior needs. I had to learn the tiers (Tier 1, 2, and 3) in order to be able to identify how to meet my students and mentees negative behavior needs and change them to positive behaviors

Introduction

through RTI interventions. I try to provide a safety net before these students fail academically and fall by the wayside. My passion for young people is represented in a gritty way as it is not always easy to meet the needs of those I have mentored right away. I have had to persevere through some trying times with students who were a process to change their negative behaviors that they were always used to. In other words, students who love to cut up and show out against teachers and administration are usually sent to me to help them. It was not always easy. Some did not change right away, however, through love, compassion, showing that I care, persevering interventions, teaching and positive leadership; along with helping them find their passions, and teaching them how to set short- and long-term goals, change eventually came. Change still comes to this day as I continue to persevere, help students change their negative habits and help students meet new goals and make a difference in their lives.

10. Indoor and outdoor classrooms. Providing indoor activities based on lessons and instruction that gear toward a particular subject matter. Supplying outdoor activities that relate to indoor instruction in order to allow the students to experience another side to learning in a different environment.
11. Community-based instruction and learning. Going beyond the classroom 4 walls and into the community. Providing activities to be completed in their community and at home while using virtual learning as well.

You Can Be An Overachiever Through Grit
My gifts were a life saver for me through grit. I was so multi-talented that I felt that I could win in anything no matter what it was. I loved sports and was exceptionally good at them all. I was a high achiever.

I found out in the fifth grade that I could outrun everybody at my school through "field day" events. Later, I was team captain and played varsity sports as a freshman in high school. I was in the city newspaper highlighting my outstanding stats and athletic accomplishments. I was well known locally by my school, school district and community as being a great athlete. Later as I began my teaching career, as a teacher and coach, coaching high school freshman basketball, my team was first place in district and coaching JV (Junior Varsity) Volleyball, we were second in district. There was only one thing missing, my understanding of what true grit meant in my life back then.

I participated in the AAU (Athletic Amateur Union) and the Junior Olympics; I was about nine. I also participated in the Jesse Owens Games in Los Angeles, California where I was asked to carry the torch for the opening games. The games were held at UCLA (University of California, Los Angeles). I was not expecting the Games to ask me nor even think or believe in me to accomplish such a gritty goal, but they did. I ran around the track with a crowded stadium that was full to compacity. They were all cheering for me, cheering for the moment, and cheering for the great name that it represented—"Jesse Owens" and all that he accomplished during his legacy here on earth.

I was surprised, however, honored to be called upon and I did not want to let the Games down. I did not want to let my family watching trackside down. And I did not want to let the thousands of people down who came to remember the cause and the history and the great legacy of the Jesse Owens Games.

As I ran around the track, all the hard work, dedication, motivation and true grit—the will to persevere to win, all cluttered my mind as I made the last turn of the 400 yards to finish my historical moment of carrying the torch. True grit was birthed within me, and I didn't even know it. No matter how hard my life has been, I made it. I had to persevere through many hard trials and

Introduction

tribulations. Many setbacks and undeserving circumstances that came up against me. But I made it, and I made it through by obtaining true grit. I'm sure you may be saying the same thing about your life and career.

Although my past is behind me, I still follow the word "grit" now that I am an entrepreneur, educator, author and mentor leader trying to make a difference in the lives of young people every day as the school doors open up. I speak positive words to my students and mentees each school day. I speak knowledge, instill innovation, motivation, grit and hope. I teach them to persevere through all obstacles that may come their way. I'm able to build a positive and professional relationship with them while being candid and transparent, letting them know that they can make it against all odds. This allows them to know that I am not so high and perfect. I let them know that I have made mistakes in my life that I'm not proud of, however, I made it through by getting my education and working hard to receive my bachelor's degree, three master's degrees, and now being a doctorate candidate. This is something that I never thought I could ever accomplish because I was told that I was stupid and that I was not going to be anything in life.

There were many times I was overlooked, rejected and picked over. No one believed in me but my mom, my family and a few fingers of friends. That is all I had to hold on to and I embraced every bit of them. My mom taught me to never quit and to do the best that I could with all the gifts and talents God has given to me. My mom is my inspiration as she strived to accomplish grit—persevering against all odds to provide for her children while working two and three jobs when my siblings and I were young. I learned grit at an early age and again did not even know it.

The greatest opportunity I made in my life was to make a difference in the lives of each student that I could. I want to help change the mentality of our youth who do not believe in themselves and are victims of their negative living conditions. I do not want students to fail because of their academic struggle, the color of their skin, gender, creed, disability, living conditions, or the culture or background they came from. This is why I started a mentoring program at my school—to reach as many young people as possible.

As I work with Tier 1, 2, and 3 students, at-risk and mobility rate students of all races, I want them to know that just because they may not have as many opportunities as other students who came up in better financially stable neighborhoods, and just because they make a mistake in life, doesn't mean that it is the end of the world, it just means that they have another opportunity to get it right, work a little harder and make something great of themselves with a story to tell and inspire others.

The Power of Grit in the Classroom, School and Community came to me when the pandemic struck our city and we received stay-at-home orders. Many people do not realize the power of grit that lies within them. I came across the word "grit" while looking on the internet for something else as this word caught my eye. I have always been the type of person who if I did not know how to spell a word, I would go straight to the internet and the dictionary and find out. Now days you can speak to Google, and it will look up anything for you. It's amazing how times and technology has changed.

The word "grit" stood out at me, and I rushed to look up the meaning. As I read the meaning—a person with passion and perseverance, I found out they set goals and follow through to complete them. A person who has grit works really hard to follow through on commitments has true grit. Although it is not a word you hear every day or often to none, it is a powerful word that needs attention.

The Power of Grit in the Classroom, School and Community was birthed, and I challenge you to do your research on the word "grit" after reading this book, and how it applies to your life, school campus and classroom. Students show grit every day on your campus and in your classrooms and you may not have realized it. Believe it or not,

Introduction

there are some students, teachers and administrators who live to be successful in grit every day of their lives and they may not even realize it.

Grit is life or death in poor neighborhoods. It is a lifesaver to some who have never had anything in life. They work hard and persevere until they achieve the goal that they are seeking after. Some never get that chance. Students come to school everyday persevering through some hard challenges, better yet still trying to reach their dreams and goals. I push students to not give up and to work through grit against all odds. I believe in all students. I do not give up on students no matter how severe their situation looks, how detrimental their academics appear, and how negative their past has been. I'm certainly not perfect in what I do each school day, however, I am very humble to be given an opportunity and a career that provides each teacher, staff, parent, administrator, school principal, stakeholder, and superintendent an opportunity to instill true grit—the power of passion and perseverance in the lives of many students as much as possible. I believe anybody can change and become the person they dream of becoming in life. I have personally witnessed this with students and people I have mentored, counseled and coached throughout the years.

True grit is every athlete's best friend and every coach's dream, especially when they work hard to coach an underdog winning team that nobody believes in nor believe could ever win. *The Power of Grit in the Classroom, School and Community* will open up your eyes to see a whole new dimension of the power that lies within you for greatness through grit and the power it possesses.

As I shared some of my story not for amusement, however, to show the gritty life I have been through, the accomplishments that I have come from, and the overachiever I have become. There is still yet more to accomplish as I look forward to achieving it.

As you read *The Power of Grit in the classroom, School, and Community,* I encourage you to become a gritty person and strive to accomplish your passion; and persevere until the end through setting and meeting short-term and long-term goals even when obstacles and hurtles may come your way.

What Does it Mean to Have Grit?

Grit is not a word that you often hear about. Grit is defined, as Angela Duckworth, (2016) adds, *"perseverance and passion for long-term goals."* Grit involves enduring challenges that a student, parent, teacher or principal may face in life, and not giving up, but working toward being successful against all odds. He or she maintains effort and interest over the years despite failure, adversity, and high or low hills in any progress they may have attempted to make. To have grit means to have courage and to exemplify strength of the character you possess. A person who shows true grit has passion and perseverance. You show passion toward your students and persevere when you do not see progress right away in them. A person who works really hard to follow through on what he or she says they are going to do or follows through on commitments has true grit. Goals are set and followed through. Grit applies to academic learning, homework assignments, co-worker collaboration, student projects, friendships, relationships, student, teacher parent, and principal fears.

> **To have grit means to have courage and to exemplify strength of the character you possess.**

Stephanie Franklin

I think of my students *(in my engineering class)*, mentees *(from my mentor program)* and the school campus students through the STEAM Education I have visioned and coordinate each year, as I have had the opportunity to make a difference in their lives and have personally witnessed their success either by them stopping me down the hallway saying, *"I had fun and learned a lot at your STEAM FEST,"* or by bumping into them at the mall and having not seen them in years, or at the gas station putting gas in my vehicle, as one of them recognized me and came up to me to tell me that he listened to my motivating words to help him and the students; and that he took every word and applied it to his life and now he's a successful engineer. Or students coming up to the school to tell me thank you, or just some who comes by my classroom just to say thank you.

How do you as a student, teacher, administrator, staff member, business owner, leader, co-worker, coach, athlete, college student, high school or college grad get grit? If you lack passionate and persevering abilities, you can get grit in these five ways:

1. Find something that strikes or fascinates your interests and pursue it without giving up.
2. Create a routine and practice and train hard and work to get better every day.
3. Connect through your faith to reach higher for the purpose that you're trying to pursue.
4. Cultivate hope. You gotta' want it.
5. Surround yourself with people who are going in the same direction and believe in what you are trying to accomplish. Those are called gritty people and gritty friends.

Through grit, you can carefully craft each lesson and deliver them with passion, perseverance and commitment. However, the question is asked: How do you know that your students are learning what you are teaching them? Below are six points that will let you know if they are on it or not:

1. Formulate a summative assessment within your lessons.
2. Push your students toward critical thinking skills.
3. Provide a self-assessment check. Check for understanding and evaluate yourself through instructional domains 1-4.
4. Make sure your authentic assessments are accurate.
5. Your project-based learning is successful.
6. A Framework for teaching- using the T-TESS Rubric accountability as you teach alongside the rubric—Planning, Instruction, Learning Environment and Professional Practices and Responsibilities. Your goal should be to be a "Distinguished" leader every day in your classroom as well as your school campus.
7. I have included the four domains in the back of the book for you to follow and for added additional understanding.

As the world is ever changing at the blink of our eyes, teachers and principals seek to keep up much as possible. Various engaging instructions, activities and technology are added to the schools and classroom gritty climate for learning. Teachers and principals run to incorporate these eight points of important variables:

1. Innovative Classroom Practices.
2. Teacher Self-Care.
3. Networking Skills (Core and CTE (Career & Technical) elective courses).
4. Professional Developments (for students and teachers).
5. Technology (physical in class learning and virtual learning).
6. Digital Leadership.
7. Climate for Learning and Change.
8. Integration of the Subjects.

I am providing a scenario that pertains to this chapter that may help you as a teacher in your classroom and/or administrator on your

Stephanie Franklin

school campus. You may have or will encounter this situation and need a positive breakthrough on how to handle it effectively for the success of all students and your campus.

Scenario 1:

Jessica is a 9th grader at Sims High School. She is in Mr. Grimes P.E. class, and they are preparing to go rock climbing at Winterworld Rock Climbing. The students conquer most projects and are not afraid to conquer this huge undertaking project. Jessica is the ringleader. Jessica is usually the first to get done with all in class assignments and she usually makes all A's on her assignments and test. Unlike most all the other classmates have to struggle to keep up with her.

At Winterworld it was a different story. All the other students were perfect at climbing the rocky wall all the way to the top as Jessica struggled to make it halfway up to be unsuccessful as she fell each time she tried.

She dropped to her knees and burst out crying as Mr. Grimes came to console her and asked, "Jessica, what's wrong. Are you okay?"

Jessica yelled out, "I can't make it to the top! I'm always first and can do everything right! I don't understand!"

Mr. Grimes spoke calmly to her, "I realize you are a straight 'A' student in class, but this is way different than class work, it requires you to persevere and concentrate until you make it up to the top of the wall. You not only have to think about each step up you make before taking a step as you make your way up the wall, but you also must have concentration, determination and resilience to do so. Can you do this?"

"Yes sir I can! I now see that I wasn't taking my time and concentrating before I took a step up the wall, especially when I got tired."

"Well, let's get up that wall. I know you can do it!"

The Power of Grit in the Classroom, School, and Community

Jessica got up off the floor and jumped on her first rock and on up the wall she went and made it to the top with a new attitude and determination.

This scenario shows why grit is important and should be taught in schools. Many students start out strong in the beginning of the year and as the year progresses, they go down and lose their passion, perseverance and resilience to continue strong. We must understand that there is always a "why" in students and teacher's behavior. It is okay to not understand every assignment given to them, and we as parents, teachers and administrators can teach students that. It is also okay to let students know that they will fall and make mistakes, and may not understand everything, but we should encourage them to build on those mistakes and not quit—that is grit. Jessica started strong up the wall and lost her ability to maintain, made some bad choices, but she did not quit. She bounced back and learned resilience and met her goal of getting up that rocky wall at Winterworld. We should teach our students to be just like Jessica. Students may make mistakes, however, with the teaching of grit and resilience, they can be encouraged to bounce back and meet short term and long goals in each one of their classes and within sports team if they are athletes.

Questions to Share with Your Class, Teen Group, and/or School:

The question is, was Jessica wrong for dropping to the floor when she could not make it up the wall to the top? Was Mr. Grimes wrong for going over to Jessica so soon instead allowing her to adjust and go until she made it up the wall? Should Jessica have consulted with Mr. Grimes on how to get up the wall before giving up and dropping to the floor? Did Mr. Grimes yell at Jessica or did he speak calmly to her? Should they have had a student, parent and teacher conference? Was this that serious? Did Mr. Grimes teach Jessica grit? Did she end with a gritty attitude after she made it to the top of the wall?

Stephanie Franklin

If this were you in this situation, what would you do? How would you feel or react? Write your answers below and if you are in a group, mentorship session, class or sports team talk about it with them.

The Power of Grit in the Classroom, School, and Community

Stephanie Franklin

The Power of Grit in the Classroom, School, and Community

Stephanie Franklin

Developing the Power of Grit in Your Students and in Your School

As a teacher myself, I see grit being practiced in my students every day. However, most do not realize that they are showing grit as they work hard to get each assignment completed each day. But the question I ask as I see some teachers who do not know that they are practicing grit is, why do some students manage their time with the small percentage of resources given by their teacher, whereas a few exceptional students push themselves past their limits to completion? Why do some students accomplish more than other students as they each have the same opportunities and equal brainpower? Grit is students or individuals who share high success and achievement.

> Grit takes place when a high achieving student sets him or herself apart from everyone else.

Grit takes place when a high achieving student sets him or herself apart from everyone else. They work harder, they put in more time than the norm, and they are always first in line. For example, I had a student who was always the first one to make it to class. He was on time with no complaints. He was always the first one to complete all of my assignments as he was successful with making A's on every

39

assignment. So, one day I asked him, "why are you so dedicated to my class?" And he answered, "Because I wanna' be successful one day." He showed all qualities of Grit—perseverance and passion for long-term goals. This would be great if all of our students were this way. Well, guess what? They can. I've learned, and are still learning, to just keep it simple. Do not try to invent a wheel that is working already. Students learn by example, and they learn by seeing and hearing. Visual and site. They learn best when teachers are not trying to be too deep, meaning they are trying to put too much in the lesson and lose students because they bore them with way too much talking that doesn't make sense; nor does it apply to the lesson they are attempting to teach. Again, just keep it simple and straight to point.

How do you as a teacher or principal develop grit within your students and school environment? Remember, it is important each day to work through challenges that may arise that are beyond your control. Maintain effort and a passionate attitude and interest throughout the school year despite failure, adversity, and up roaring hills you may encounter inside of school, outside of school and in your personal life. Believe it or not, what you go through outside of school affects your progress or actions while at work—in school. Grit cannot be successful when you are in a state of defeat. Believe me, your students know when you're not your normal self. They know when something is wrong or when you are not motivated with a mind of helping to make them successful. Grit is important for students in school as well as in life. Many times, what you say and what you teach each student affects them when they leave the school each day. Either it affects them in a positive way, or it affects them in a negative way. It is important to always remain professional, even when you want to relax a little with your students because there is no disruptive behavior at the time. I have seen teachers and principals become way too comfortable with students, and when a sudden crises or trauma arises, they are not prepared and cannot handle the consequence. Perseverance is needed to help in this area or professionalism. Building perseverance in yourself and in your students are not always easy as it seems. Perseverance comes with persistence. Being persistent each day is the key to winning with grit. You must be persistent and not movable or changeable. One day you're up and the next day your down, the next day you're on fire and ready to win and make a difference in the lives of students, then the next day when someone says something negative about your teaching style of how weak you are as a teacher or principal, your persistency runs right out the door with anger (you're ready to fight with all you got), regret (regret that you ever became a teacher or principal), and hurt (can't believe they thought that way of you or said that about you).

Although we live in a world filled with things that are convenient for us like, smart TV's, ATMs, fast speed internet access, social media, video calls, texting, group chats, video games, internet and TV voice recognitions, this has demobilized and diminished the progress, work ethic and perseverance in our students' learning and success learning.

How do we as parents, teachers, counselors, assistant principals, and principals encourage the following strategies or perseverance, resilience and persistency in our children or students?

1. Talk to your child or student(s) about the importance of keeping a positive attitude and perseverance and persistency each day. Students underscore how valuable this trait is in order to be successful in life, school, and in the workplace when that time permits.
2. Turn a problem into a picture. Something they each can get a visual—they can see. "Drawing by modeling." For example, students turn math problems into a picture or something they can visually see, which helps them as they are engaged and using both sides of their brain.
3. Keep it simple and understandable. Use problems or lessons that they can accomplish. Your goal is to help your students

to be successful, not being the ol' grinch who doesn't want them to learn and try every way possible to keep them from it because you're upset about their negative behavior.

4. Share your "why" and then the "you can." Many times, we fail to inspire our students because we are too afraid to be transparent or to share the relevance of the lesson or problem. We are afraid to share our story or share success stories of how we overcame obstacles in our own careers and in life that got us where we are now. Children and students need this as it helps them to know that since you overcame all of your obstacles and made it, so can I. Making a difference in the lives of children and students should be the "why" and the "you can" of every teacher and principal who shows up for work each day. Even when at times you do not feel like going.

5. Grouping. Embody a community of grouping your students together. Students love to problem solve as they work with their peers to get the assignment completed. Myself as a teacher call this teambuilding in my classroom. I teach on this method all the time and find it to work successfully in my classroom with my students. Students love working together with those who share the same like work ethics. It pushes the best out of them. It brings the grit out of them as it helps them to push toward short term and long-term goals and complete them. When keeping students alone, it can make them stagnated and feel intimidated, isolated, inferior and alone.

6. I love competition but in the right way. I love to pair, group or put my students in competitions that causes them to work together and use their individual strengths. I have learned that when students use their strengths, they do not feel unsure of themselves. However, remove all barriers that keep them from being successful and sets a positive atmosphere and environment for learning. It's like being in a basketball locker room after winning a game. Everybody's celebrating

their success all at the same time and there is no room for defeat.

7. Reward your child or students. Encourage them that hard work pays off. Reward them when they're in competition as your goal is not to teach them to compete as a negative innuendo or with sore losing. However, compete with a reward of success within a lesson or task in the end.
8. Boost your child or student's self-esteem with words of, "you can achieve" rather than words of defeat like "you'll never be nothing in life because you're stupid and can't understand nothing." Bring out the best in your child or student(s) as you encourage them to persevere on a challenging task or assignment. And encourage them to persevere to come to school when it's slightly raining and cold outside at their bus stop.

Can a student learn to have girt? How do you teach it? You will learn how to teach grit in chapter 4.

Why is Grit Important for Students?

Grit is important as it drives and delivers achievement and success. It independently goes beyond a student's talent or intelligence of contribution. Without grit, a student's talent may be considered as just a talent or unmerited selfless potential. Without effort, grit becomes lifeless. However, with effort, grit becomes a skill that develops and leads to the success in each student, or school, or campus, or faculty, or staff, or company employees, or within a community or family.

Grit is also important to meet the needs of students. It helps with differentiating instruction and meeting various needs of students.

Grit is important for each student who desires to go beyond high school graduation on into college admittance. Colleges want well qualified and a strong diverse class student body. Students who demonstrate grit is more likely to succeed while in stressful times of facing challenges and adversity in their lives.

So, why is grit important for students? It is what drives achievement and success. It is important because it goes beyond just the ordinary of showing off your talent with no success or goal in mind to accomplish. Moreover, it is the ability to persevere and do well and thrive through obstacles and potential setbacks. One year I had a student who came to school with a positive attitude every day. It wasn't one day that she did not have a smile on her face. In fact, each day she came in my classroom she said good morning and asked me how my morning was going. One day I was talking to my students and began to share some life-long wisdom and out of nowhere, this young lady says that although she's going through a touch battle with being in foster care and pressing to come to school every day with the struggle of wanting to drop out, she comes anyway because she wants to graduate and make something great of herself. She did not want to be a statistic or a drop out. This is persevering through hard times and delivering achievement through a positive attitude and a will to win no matter what it looks like. Therefore, grit is important for students.

Grit is also important to meet the needs of students. It helps with differentiating instruction and meeting various needs of students. I will show you how I differentiate for my students individually and by groups (team building) below:

- I encourage thinking at various levels of Bloom's taxonomy.
- I encourage thinking at various levels from the Teaching for Learning Charts *(found below)*.
- I use a variety of instructional delivery methods to address different learning styles.
- I break assignments into smaller, more manageable parts that include structured directions for each part.
- I choose broad instructional concepts and skills that lend themselves to understanding at various levels of complexity.
- I develop activities that target auditory, visual, and kinesthetic learners.
- I establish stations in the classroom, in the computer lab, and in the industrial lab for inquiry-based, independent learning activities and projects.

- I create activities that vary in level of complexity and degree of abstract thinking required.
- I use flexible grouping to group and regroup students based on factors including content, ability, and assessment results.

FOR ALL COURSES

Our Teaching and Learning Strategy
What are we trying to achieve for your education?

Highest Quality
We always seek to maintain, improve and develop our standards of teaching, learning, assessment as well as your support and guidance. In so doing we strive to preserve the integrity, validity and currency of our teaching provision. External rigorous quality management systems gave us the highest possible mark thus rating us among the very best in the UK.

Enthusiasm
We aim to convey a culture for enthusiasm for the subject matter and for scientific enquiry throughout all programmes in the Department. It is our belief that enthusiastically delivered courses are more likely to lead to enthusiastic, motivated and successful students and graduates.

Innovation
We are constantly seeking to maintain a mindset of teaching innovation that is encouraged in many forms e.g. through the design of our curriculum. Staff have been successful in winning teaching innovation awards and the Department has a considerable activity involved in research into teaching in the biosciences with a publication record in its own right.

Research-inspiration
We seek to develop a positive learning culture by fostering a close relationship between research and teaching where you can learn in a research atmosphere. The biosciences are fast-moving and research-inspired by their nature; thus we strive to provide you with a learning experience in a research-driven atmosphere. We believe that if we engage and motivate you in this way you are more likely to complete the course of study, explore data and concepts in an independent manner and fulfil (or exceed) our expectations of your ability.

FOR ALL COURSES

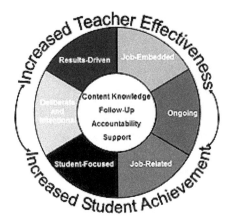

How Do You Teach Grit?

When one thinks of the word "grit", he or she may think that it is a slang for the use of another word or phrase or eating a bowl of grits may come to mind. Well, grit doesn't mean eating grits or is it used as a slang. Grit, in fact, is a very important word regarding the success of our schools, our students, our staff, our teachers, our principals, and anyone who has the passion and perseverance to be successful in life. Successful people throughout history, in sports, business, music, science, technology, engineering, fine arts, and in math have used grit to achieve their goals.

So, I know you're saying, get to the point. And asking, "How do I teach my students grit?" I can only answer by how I teach my students. This is how I teach my students grit. I am not only a teacher, but I am also a life coach, a coach (outside of school), a personal trainer, and a mentor. I mentor students on a daily basis as I also mentor an afterschool mentoring program. Within these very important aspects in my

> *Grit doesn't mean eating grits or is used as a slang. Grit, in fact, is a very important word regarding the success of our schools, our students, our staff, our teachers, our principals, and anyone who has the passion and perseverance to be successful in life.*

career and life that I hold in high regard, I teach grit to my students and mentees to help them:

1. Find their purpose whether career wise or what they are passionate about in life.
2. Create a <u>vision board</u> (Use poster board) regarding what they want to become, and where they see themselves in life years later; and shoot for it.
3. Create a <u>vision folder</u> (Use a 1 or 2 inch 3-ring binder) that helps them create their vision for their career and educational goals. I try to have meaningful conversations that help bring authentic conversations to my classroom and program.
4. Create an SEL (Social and Emotional Learning) Folder (Use a 1 or 2 inch 3-ring binder) that helps them with meaningful age-appropriate social and emotional conversations that help them to vent and identify what bothers them. It also helps them with empathy as it shows them how to have compassion and understanding towards other students, staff and teachers. It helps them to manage stress and increase self-control, and to build interpersonal skills and build better relationships as they strive through school and through life.
5. By giving them examples and stories about famous people who have exemplified grit in their careers and how they worked hard to get where they are today. I call these people, "gritty famous people." They each have persevered, showed resilience and their success shows it. As most of my mentees are classified as Tier 3 teens who have existing academic, social, emotional, and/or behavior problems, I seek to find leaders and famous people who were once on their level and did not give up but came out and made something great of themselves. You can also use this method as it has been, and

still is very successful for me not only in my classroom, but also within my after-school mentoring program.
6. Through instructional practices within my lessons. When they fail a particular assignment, they do not have to feel like a failure, they can study hard and try again and pass with a good grade.
7. By conducting one on one grit interviews with my students. I find out what makes them want to quit. I find out what makes them want more out of their courses and my program. I find out how I can reach them. Lastly, I find out what activities I can provide for them to help them grow and help them advance within my course of study.
8. Try "the Grit Pie" Exercise (see the grit pie on the next page).

Self-perception matters as it relates to teaching students about the impact of negative and positive thoughts and beliefs on their ability to succeed. Students who have developed a habit of negative talk will have a hard time exercising grit. However, as they learn to speak positive and create positive traits, grit will be successful in their studies and within their lives.

The Grit Pie above represents an obstacle the student is facing. The pie itself is the problem. Each slice of the pie represents a cause of the problem. What is the solution of the grit pie? There are two ways to foster grit in your classroom and with each student:

1. Teach your students about the impact of thoughts and beliefs on their ability to succeed in life, making the right career choices, and how to build culture among other students (share where each other are from, learn from each of their pasts, create culture that aligns with their core values, complement each other, work together and work as a team). Students have developed a habit of telling themselves that they are bad at everything and will not amount to anything. Failure is inevitable and will have a hard time with grit.

2. Teach your students how to work on their emotions. Intervention activities are great when it comes to helping to control a student's emotional outburst. For example, a student may burst out and yell at another student, "You make me sick! I hate you because you put me down like my dad puts me down!" Or try this one as a student may yell at the teacher when they are really yelling at their parents who disciplines them and gives them a directive, "Stop telling me what to do! You're just like my parents! I'm tired of everybody telling me what to do!" So, the goal here is to help your students talk out what bothers them instead of using other reasons to take their pain and frustration out on. Teach them to use their past pains and frustrations as steppingstones and use them as strengths to succeed and not fail. It is easy to send them to the principal's office with a

referral or a call home complaining about their negative behavior and/or outbursts, but first try these steps before going that far.

Here are some classroom activities that build culture within your classroom:

1. Create an opening message to your students that welcomes them each day. Show that you care about how their morning or day is going. For example, ask how their day or morning is going. Ask how they feel. Create a warmup that gets them going.
2. Model gritty behavior that fosters a heart of passion that is contagious to your students and not complaining, dragging and boring.
3. Create gritty assignments and warmups that creates culture. When you as the teacher or principal deliver curriculum to your students, students will gravitate the opportunity to construct meaning of what is being taught to them.
4. Expect learning outcomes—breakdown your assignments into manageable parts, structure directions, and example planning of the blueprint—the plan or outline.
5. Establish your content objectives that should be clearly stated on your dry erase board or chalkboard and wall. You should establish those objectives so that they are understandable and not too deep to understand for your students. This should happen on every school campus. Many times, teachers tend to focus more on teaching the content, rather than making sure that each student understands the content. Your ultimate goal is to create an assignment that allows your students to win and understand the subject matter of the lesson, rather than make the assignment way to confusing and have the students yelling, "I do not understand! This is way too

hard!" And they all get bad grades. This should not ever be the goal of a successful teacher.

Every school is different and unique within its own share of issues. Every student learner comes to school with a will to learn or a will to act up. Each have their own share of challenges, strengths, emotional needs, concerns, and cultural backgrounds. Each class within the school is different and demonstrates a uniqueness because of what the teacher brings each day within his or her classroom. You as the teacher is in total control of your classroom and have the power to make each student feel comfortable and a part of the class or feel uncomfortable and want to disturb the rest of the students. If you are not in control of your classroom and a student becomes uncomfortable and begins to disturb your classroom, this means that you did not take control and now cannot teach your classroom effectively because you have to deal with the disturbance. You may say that it is the student's fault, when in fact, it is the teacher who did not exercise his or her power to take control of his or her classroom; and make the students feel comfortable. This also relates to building a classroom environment for learning. Each student's needs are met, and learning is inevitable. You can build a classroom full of compassion and create a sense of relationship at the very beginning that is based on respect and trust. Building a relationship with your students is very important and they really do matter. So, you may be asking, "how do I build a relationship with my students?" I will answer by asking you to ask yourself what is the need of each of your students? And follow that question by answering yourself by saying, "I will do my best to meet the needs of each of my students."

So, in a nutshell, how do you embed grit as a means to build culture in your classroom? I will answer by saying to:
1. MODEL gritty behavior by showing compassion and passion for each student no matter the color, nationality, creed, or outer appearance.

2. ESTABLISH A VISION daily in your classroom and communicate it to your students daily. This will give them a sense of direction and a daily short-term goal to reach.
3. SET HIGH EXPECTATIONS with those daily visions and goals you have established.
4. CREATE a competitive positive environment with your students.
5. CREATE an environment where students share where they come from and feel comfortable by sharing their cultural backgrounds as this will allow them to respect and understand each other better. This can minimize a lot of behavior issues, backbiting and bullying.
6. CREATE study groups and discussion among your students.
7. PROVIDE ongoing coaching with your students to improve performance and meet their needs.
8. GIVE incentives for good behavior. You can never go wrong with this one. Every student love incentives whether it is for good behavior, or for their hard work and perseverance paying off.
9. MENTOR your students who may be struggling. Do not dump them off on the campus mentoring program or counselors, or SEL Coordinator you can mentor your students yourself and let them know you care; and reach out to show them how to be successful in your classroom and in life.

Here are more ways to tackle grit in your classroom and in your school:
1. Read to your students about grit.
2. Hold study groups and discussions.
3. Discuss different trends to your students.
4. Share examples about grit.
5. Help your students to develop a growth mindset.

6. Foster safe circumstances within your school that promote and encourage grit.

Take a look at some sample grit charts and posters on the next page that intrigued me. I encourage you to create your own grit chart and posters for your classroom and for your school. Also, I challenge you to create a lesson with your students by assigning them to create their own grit chart and poster. I have provided the examples of the grit charts so you can use as only examples of how your students can create their own. DO NOT COPY THE GRIT CHARTS AS YOU SEE THEM. Only use them as examples to create your own with your students or school, and when your students begin to plan how they will design and complete their own grit charts and posters. You and your students or school can make a grit chart to target your goals.

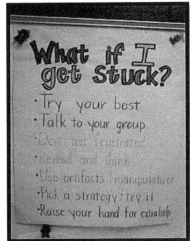
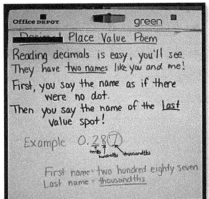

Stephanie Franklin

When your students or school have completed your Grit Posters, you all can hang them on your classroom doors, on your classroom walls, on your main hallway walls on your campus so that teachers and staff can view them and be encouraged by your students and what grit goals to follow each day.

Create Your Own Grit Chart Below:

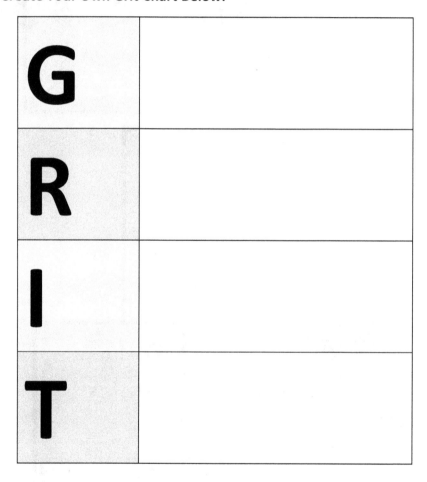

What is Grit and Growth Mindset?

Grit is passion and perseverance towards reaching a long-term goal. Resilience is the optimism to keep bouncing back from failure. Both traits for success are rooted in a growth mindset, and everyone—you as a teacher, your students, as a principal, as a staff member working with students on a daily basis can learn, develop, and build resilience and grit for the success; and as you fulfill the needs of the students.

So, whether you work at a Title 1 or Tier 1 school with students who have negative behavior or SEL (Social Emotional Learning) challenges, or a perfect school that has no challenges, grit and growth mindset applies to both.

> **Growth Mindset is believed to be developed through dedication and hard work—using your brain is just the starting point.**

Growth Mindset is believed to be developed through dedication and hard work—using your brain is just the starting point. This atmosphere creates a love for learning and a resilience that is essential for great success among students, athletes, coaches, teachers and people. For example, in growth mindset, you believe "Anyone can be good at anything. Skill only comes from practice." Growth mindset is the belief that it is possible to increase intelligence levels, talents, and abilities. For example, students often want to give up when things get hard. They may run from mistakes, challenges, failures, or approach success differently to their classmates with growth mindset.

As I did research, I found that there is an association between a student's growth mindset and grit. As an educator, I was curious to know and to understand the relationship of a student who exemplifies growth mindset and grit to better nurture my students learning in my classroom. I always look for ways to better advance my student's learning. This is what it's all about—always meeting the needs of students at all costs; and looking for ways to grow as a teacher.

How does growth mindset relate to grit? One must find out what grit is and what growth mindset is and put them both together. Grit is a characteristic that can be found in a student with a growth mindset. A student who demonstrates grit is known to be steadfast with the ability to show passion and perseverance with great effort toward meeting a specific goal. For example, a football athlete playing in a game, "I'm happy we're winning the game in the fourth quarter because we worked so hard to come back from losing in the first half." This behavior found in a student/athlete is an aspect of a growth mindset which builds a student's ability to grow within his or her emotions, hard effort toward completing a short- and long-term goal, completing and staying on top of classroom course work, within after school activities, on their job, and at home.

Can Grit Be Improved?

To answer this question, yes, grit can be improved. A student, a teacher, a staff member, or a principal can create practices to improve their grit overtime. For example, you can work on a difficult task everyday consistently until you conquer it. Another example is continuously working on a homework assignment or lesson plan that you find very difficult to come together or to get your students to understand. You may even try to finish a complicated project that seems too hard to complete. How about working on something that you find challenging will prime your mind and motivation to persevere.

As you as an educator or your students train your gritty mindset, you will increase your perseverance to stick in there when you want to quit but persevere until the end. Your grit will become greater. As an educator you can improve grit among your students by taking an approach to create a lesson plan that trains your students to exercise grit. Time your students to attempt grit among each other within a daily warm up or an assignment and allow them time to exercise the necessary characteristics of grit in your classroom.

Increase Resilience to Any Labels and Stereotypes of Any Kind
As you nurture your students or school with growth mindset, stereotypes cannot disrupt your student's effort and focus. When your students stand up to stereotypes, it becomes much easier to fight back intelligently without consequences. It also helps them to fight back with their intelligence, rather with their hands and mouth. If the students in your school are fighting every day or on a regular basis, it is important to go back to the drawing board with behavior interventions that will not only hold them accountable, but the staff as well.

All students are not wrong. Since none of us are perfect, there may be times the teacher, staff or the principal may be at fault. It is okay to show students the consequences for negative behavior. There is always a way to be successful since it is important to help students be successful and meet their needs.

Creating a climate and culture for learning on every campus is very important to impart each day before the school doors open. Notice I said before? I say this because preparation is important. Just as if the staff, as a TEAM, is preparing to play during a sporting game, the staff should prepare for the school day just like this—as a

TEAM. How do we prepare as a TEAM? By showing up early to work. By waiting for instructions from leadership and your principal. By collaborating with your co-workers. By helping and lending a hand when you're not asked to. By working together as you take your individual assignments seriously—holding yourself accountable—how you treat one another (remove or shun away from co-worker brawls), how you treat the students (remove or shun away from judging race, gender, appearance, and/or negative personalities). By not making campus expectations way too difficult for the students, teachers, and staff to follow. And lastly, by making school expectations and rules as your major counter point is to score big and come out successful each day.

Everybody must be serious about teaching. If teaching is a battle or unbearable for you, either you need to go back to the drawing board with additional trainings, professional developments, workshops, SEL (Social Emotional Learning) breathers and interventions, and/or have your appraiser monitor and review you teaching your class; and afterwards set up an appointed time to show you what you need to work on or any areas needing to perfect.

Students need excited teachers who love their job. Not teachers who dread coming to work and pull-on students who feel just the opposite—they want to learn and are ready to win with learning in your class each school day. The goal here is to make things go smooth all day long with students reporting to class on time, smooth transitions between class changes (if apply to you), teachers guiding their students where they need to go, teachers standing at their classroom doors greeting their students between class transitions, principals overseeing the needs of the building and student's needs and behavior, curriculum is being taught at a high level that makes students excited about learning and teachers excited about teaching, hallways are filled with student achievement and campus expectations on the walls, signs with directions on the walls that give students instructions on how and where they need to go, do, and operate.

The school day should be filled with success on all levels every day. I have found that students are very structured and need to be lead as they wait for instructions and for their campus leaders to lead by example. If leadership is not taking place on your campus, campus improvement must come as quick as possible before students and the campus get out of hand. Also, if this is not taking place within your teaching career, and nothing and no one can change you or your heart about being successful on your campus, with your students and in your classroom, then a career change may be appropriate.

As challenges are abundant, resilience is vital for success on the school campus and in a student's and teacher's lives. There is an impact on a student's mindset within their resilience in the face of their academics and social challenges. For example, when a student struggles with their schoolwork or homework determines whether they give up or embrace the problem and persistently work hard to overcome it. And when students feel victimized, harassed or excluded by their peers determines whether they seek revenge through their aggression, or think of more productive ways to handle the solution to the problem. With resilience, students responding to positive challenges is crucial for the success of all students in school, the community and in their lives. We must ask, what causes it? And what can be done to increase it in our students, in every classroom, on every campus, and in every school district? Two important issues that educators face in impacting student's mindsets are the impact of victimization and peer exclusion, which is a very hard subject to address. However, when it is successful, it makes the student body much meaningful and allows them freedom to get active in whatever school activity and career they are seeking and promotes a positive high self-esteem.

Stephanie Franklin

Here are critical elements to adhere to—identifying inhouse and outhouse school regulations, expectations and rules:

Add positive schoolwide expectations and post them around the school campus-

1. Areas to post would be the main entrance where everyone arrives, in each classroom, hallways, main hallway(s), student centers, the library, cafeteria, gym, and front office.
2. Behavioral expectations posted on walls, hallways, classrooms, the library, gym, and front office.

Accountability and expectations apply to all students, staff and administrators-

1. The principal, teachers, and staff have communicated the expectations to all students and staff.

   -School rules created and posted on school campus and announced at faculty meetings.

2. Behavioral rules and expectations are posted in the areas with high behavioral problems.

Staff feedback and involvement in school rules and expectations-

1. Are teachers, staff and the administrative staff involved in providing feedback and developing and following school rules and expectations at your school? Read the example of how it should be on the school campus.

Example

Inhouse—How the school functions inside the school

students reporting to class on time, smooth transitions between class changes (if apply to you), teacher's guiding their students where they need to go, principals overseeing the needs of the building and student's needs and behavior, curriculum is being taught at a high level that makes students excited to learn and teachers excited to teach.

Outhouse—How the school functions outside of the school

Bus ramp teacher duty—teachers are on their duty post monitoring the students transitions to their buses, car riders, to tutoring or to after school activities, teachers working as a team, principals are overseeing the staff and students moving along to their buses, cars or after activities smoothly.

Stephanie Franklin

After reading the Inhouse and Outhouse example, write down if this is happening on your school campus. If not, or if so, explain.

Is this happening on your campus? Please explain if so or if not.

_____
_____
_____
_____
_____
_____
_____
_____
_____
_____
_____

What are you doing to change it?

_____
_____
_____
_____
_____
_____
_____
_____
_____
_____
_____
_____

Do you care if it changes for the better? If so or if not, why?

Are you on a leadership committee on your campus? If yes, what is your role to make change or help toward it? If not, explain.

Stephanie Franklin

Identifying Inhouse and Outhouse School Regulations, Expectations and Rules-

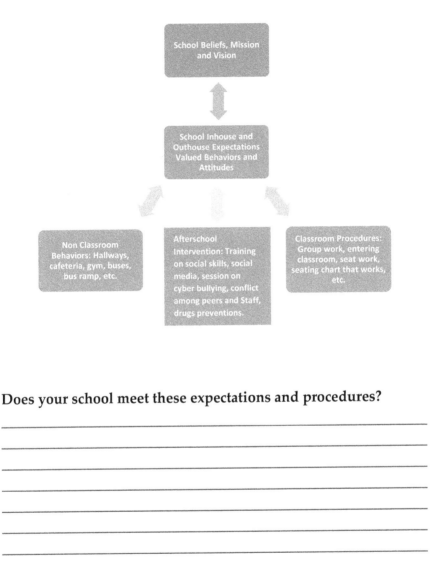

Does your school meet these expectations and procedures?

_____
_____
_____
_____
_____
_____
_____
_____
_____
_____
_____
_____

Stephanie Franklin

The Positive Weight Must Always Out-Weigh Negative Behavior in Any School and District-

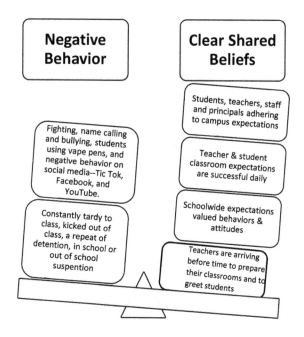

When the scale is weighed down on the positive side, there is little to no room for mess ups, negative behavior, or campus confusion.

Having a growth mindset can significantly help your students and/or school to overcome any misconceptions that may hinder their optimal performance in your classroom and in your school. There are times when female students may struggle to perform academically in science, english or math rather than male students as a result of competitive stereotypes. I have learned in my years of teaching that female students are not any less than male students. They each have the same opportunity to learn. It is what you put into it, is what will come out of it. For example, a top GPA (grade point average), top of the class academically, straight A's on the report card, AB Honor Roll, excellent conduct, awards and incentives for good behavior campus wide, student highlight (academically and/or athletically), and positive shout outs in after school activities (athletics, band, choir, art club, engineering club, S.T.E.A.M. club and theater arts) due to hard work paying off.

Important Definition to Remember
PBIS- Stands for Positive Behavior Interventions Systems. It is a three-tiered, research -based framework designed by each school, containing fundamental elements for increasing positive behavior and decreasing negative behavior. It establishes a social culture, and the behavior supports needed to improve social, emotional, behavioral, and academic outcomes for all students.

Two Types of Mindsets
Principals at this day and time must be aware of the characteristics of both types of mindsets and build a culture in which all members of the staff are lifelong learners, who will facilitate continuous improvement of the pedagogical skills, build instructional practice, and increase student achievement.

There are two types of growth mindsets: Growth and Fixed. There is a difference between Growth and Fixed.

Growth Mindset believes that ability can change as a result of effort, perseverance, and practice. You may hear a student say, "Math is hard, but if I keep trying and studying, I can get better at it." Students with growth mindsets see mistakes as ways to learn, embrace challenges, and persist in the face of setbacks.

Fixed Mindset is where students believe their basic abilities, their intelligence, their talents, are just fixed traits. Whereas with growth mindsets students understand that their talents and abilities can be developed through effort, good teaching, persistence.

Building a Positive School Culture and Climate Through Grit and Growth Mindset

Investing in students and building positive relationships with them applies to building a positive culture and climate for learning. I'll share this story of one year I had a student who always had his head hanging low while all the other students were eager and ready to learn. I had to tell him to pick his head up as he did as I told him as if he wanted to be motivated to learn but just somehow couldn't keep it up.

> *Investing in students and building positive relationships with them applies to building a positive culture and climate for learning.*

Each day before I began my lessons, I always give my students a big "good morning" and give them a motivating pep talk that brings them alive and ready to learn. They always seem to look forward to it and would let me know when I would forget. I sometimes share things that I saw on the news the night before or whatever comes to my mind. However, on this particular day, I was encouraging the students to be grateful for their parents or guardians they have and not to take them for granted. I spoke a little about when I was their age my family did not have much money to get the school supplies my siblings and I needed for our classes, and I would be embarrassed because I didn't have the supplies nor the boldness to tell the teacher in order to get my assignments completed. I would tell them if they had parents who had good jobs with a high paying income, they should be grateful. I encouraged the students who were in the same boat I was in when I was young, that I would help them get the supplies that they need.

Immediately, I noticed the boy raise his head up and smiled. He yelled out, "I don't have no supplies!"

Everybody stopped and looked his way as I softly responded back to him, "just ask your parents."

He responded back to me, "my mom is unemployed."

I softly said, "ask your dad."

He responded, "I don't have a dad. He left us when I was young, and I never seen him again."

My eyes teared up because I knew how he felt. Everybody's head went down. I immediately told him that I would help him and encouraged him and the rest of the students to lift up their heads, and to be encouraged and to use what seem like a defeat in their lives as a steppingstone to work harder to get their education, to make something great of themselves; and one day they may have an opportunity at helping their families financially. I told him that he could one day become a great father to his own children, if so choose, and help them to be successful through school. He and some of the other students smiled in agreement and teared up a little. But after that day, I did not have another problem out of him hanging his head down. Better yet, when he came in my classroom, he had more enthusiasm than I did and was ready to learn against all the odds in his life and I boosted him up even more.

He shared who he was at the time (building culture) and resilience and the optimism to keep bouncing back from failure (showing grit); and having the passion to keep coming to school against what could have been a major defeat in his life (dropping out). By sharing this true story, I built a positive climate for learning and a lasting relationship with my students to understand where they come from as they each understood where I was coming from—building a positive culture climate for learning. I have learned that it is okay to be moderately transparent with your students because it lets them know that if you can come out of a defeated situation in your own life and make it, so can they.

Students learn best when they are comfortable with the school's environment, especially when all they see is crisis when they leave the school every day. It does not help students when the staff cannot get along. It does not help when the administration is at odds with each other. It does not help when the principal and his or her leadership team does not collaborate and there is confusion as to who is leading the school. Students pick up on the slightest things and when things are out of place, they will let you know it either by their negative behaviors, by verbal slandering choice words and by bad attitudes. It is important for every school to build or rebuild where the building has been torn down, go back to the drawing board with professional development trainings, inhouse (on campus only) workshops and exemplify a positive school culture and climate for learning.

No one is exempt from growing and getting better. Teachers, staff, principals and campus police should go through a rigorous professional development and on-campus workshop to see how to better their positions on campus, their relationship with the students and staff, how to handle crises (how to handle fighting—even when there is more than one student fighting at one time, shootings, weapons found on students, off and on campus gangs, drugs found on students or selling of drugs among them, and sex acts among the students in hidden areas on campus.

Now seeing that grit is having a passion and perseverance towards reaching a long-term goal, it is important to include grit in your everyday activities at your school. You must have a passion to reach, teach, and fulfill the needs of each student that comes through the doors of your school. There is no perfect Johnny and no stupid

Stephanie Franklin

Sally. They each mean a lot and there should not be any bias among the staff. Your primary goal should be to help your students learn and be successful in your school, classroom, and in their community. Many times, we judge by what is on the outer appearance and not by who that child actually is on the inside. A child being successful in learning has no faces. It is a privilege that should not go unnoticed. This is why constant incentives and rewards for their hard work and determination is important if you want to build a gritty environment for learning and keep them learning.

Below are some things you can create, build, or sustain in a positive school culture:

1. Invest in your students (reward them when they do good)
2. Build relationships with them. Do not be afraid to be transparent. They need to know that you are not perfect and that you made some mistakes when you were their age, but you did not give up, you made it through it and made a change to better yourself and encourage them to do the same.
3. Have a shared vision. Help them build a vision board or a vision folder. Something that they can hope for and work toward. Many times, when there is no vision, students parish. Because they have nothing to hope for or believe in. When student parish, you can see it in their attitude. It is hard to get them to learn, do their homework, study for tests, be excited when they come to your school or classroom, and will even go as far as to pick fights or be involved in negative acts and behaviors.
4. Build student morale. If there is nothing for the students to get involved in or assemblies with guess motivating speakers, and student programs provided for them that are geared toward building them up culturally with hopeful dreams and aspirations that they can identify with, they will lash out and become hard to handle and the campus will suffer for it.

5. Be a role model and mentor and set the tone of your expectations to your students.
6. Praise and celebrate them when they do good whether as a group or individually.

Grit—A Two-Edged Sword: How It Applies to At-Risk Students and SEL (Social Emotional Learning) Students

When many at-risk students walk into your classroom or school, they each may have many hidden skeletons that are a product of their background and where they are now. They can be very intimidating if you allow to.

As I mentor and counsel at-risk students, and have for many years, I have learned that they each carry baggage from the hardship of their current situations. Some students carry the weight of their family, the criticism of not being financially stable like most other students who are not classified as at-risk, the need to fit in, self-esteem issues, dealing with stereotypes about their ethnicity, the missing father or mother, criticizing themselves and others for self-gratification, the use of drugs, involved in gangs, many different hardships from parental differences, hurts, and disappointments. As I have researched more in-depth how grit applies to at-risk students, Peterson (2015) and Golden (2017) mentions that grit could have negative consequences for students that are at-risk. These students are disregarded based on

Not tending to at-risk students' needs will take an effect on the entire campus.

their poverty status, race, mobility rate, language proficiency and disability.

Interventions and support are important for all at risk students. Unlike some believe that implementing grit within a school's curriculum whether in the classroom, campus wide or virtually, is not always the answer. There was a student whom I mentored years ago who could not pass their classes when they first started coming to me for help, and as some would say, they couldn't pass because they were not grittier enough. Well, I will say that it was not the fact that they were not grittier enough, it was the fact that some educators in general would blame the student for not being gritty, rather than take the blame for not implementing more interventions and professional developments for students with at-risk needs to be academically successful. Many school campuses struggle in this area which holds the greatest need. Not tending to at-risk students' needs will take an effect on the entire campus. Such as, experiencing fights every day, tearing up bathroom stalls and breaking mirrors, beating on walls in hysterical rages, breaking campus property such as, school doors and windows; even going as far as to beat up on teachers and administrators. Also, students walking out of classes without permission, students hanging around hallways and not respecting authority, nor abiding by campus expectations and the student handbook, and students bring contraband on campus and selling and using it.

Negative Repercussions for Gritty At-Risk Students
I have learned that it takes a village to raise a child. Everyone has a hand in it—parent, guardian, teacher, principal, friend, family member, motivating stakeholder, spiritual leader, mentors and community leaders. In order to accomplish current educational goals and be successful gritty leaders to educate all children and youth (our students), especially low-income minority children and youth; compared to schools with students who perform well, schools truly

need teachers and leaders who are talented, well-trained, and well-prepared. Not every teacher can work well with at-risk students. Each teacher, leader, mentor, and administrator have their proper place on every school campus. It takes a passionate, compassionate, loving, understanding, patient, strong, unselfish, motivating, teacher, leader, mentor, and administrator who sees the best in students to be successful in this area that is so neglected. It takes a teacher, leader, mentor, and administrator who wants to see students win, and a teacher, leader, mentor, and administrator who loves at all costs no matter the color (race), gender, or creed to work well with at-risk students and all students. It will be really hard to be successful without these qualities.

This is why it is important to carefully pick the school you choose to work at that you are comfortable. There was a time within my 20+ years in education where I met a teacher who was raised in a modern-day home with parents who had 6-figure jobs and didn't know what it meant to struggle. The teacher took a job at the Title 1 school filled with at-risks students who had never tasted a glaze donut that we so often take for granted. The teacher had such a hard time disciplining the students and stayed venting to me about them. The teacher told me they could not identify with the students, and it hurt them that they couldn't. I told them that it was important to take a job where they were comfortable and can reach the students freely without blemish. I was not encouraging them to move, I was making a general statement as it is important to set a goal to make a difference in the lives of students, instead of how much money the district offered as their <u>only</u> priority and concern. Salary is a huge factor. However, it should be the only factor. They could not understand what I was saying and failed majority of their students due to frustration of how the students treated them by not being fair on assignments and tests, so majority of the students failed and complained. Later than year the teacher was put on a growth plan and then later released because the students were near jumping on

81

them. The teacher resigned and was never heard of after that. Definitely I am not picking on those teachers who have come from two parent homes with high paying jobs, I am encouraging all teachers to apply at a school that you can excel at and feel comfortable along with the salary you are seeking.

Sadly, it is a shortage in the area of teaching at-risk students. Most teachers do not want the hassle of dealing with this area. It is very stressful and takes a toll on the teacher, especially when at-risk students do not change for the better right away. Although I'm sure the system works really hard, they struggle to recruit, train, hire, induct, develop, retain, or they strategically manage the most talent needed to accomplish this much needed goal on every campus. These shortcomings are most neglected and severe in large urban districts and in many suburban school districts.

Most at-risk students who are historically disregarded students based on race, poverty level, disability, and language proficiency lack the learning they most deserve due to miss judging the outer appearance rather the true grit talent they possess within. This is why it is not good to judge a book by its cover, however, only deal with the problem or struggle at hand. I have witnessed and have experienced working with RTI and at-risk students who eventually exemplified high academic achievement once their negative behavior was successfully lined up. Once I started believing in them, it was easy to get them to do anything. All most young people want is love. They want to know if you care. Most of the time teachers and leaders who work in this area may not become the teacher of the year, teacher of the month, recognized for every little thing, or the teacher who is always highlighted and receive numerous awards are never heard of. Teachers and administrators who are overlooked, principals who are not appreciated, these are mostly those who do the most and make a difference in the lives of students each day the school door opens are also never heard of. Of course, I am not stating that those who are highlighted are undeserving. However, I have just witnessed throughout my years in education this to be true. We must remember that it is not in what we look like to our coworkers or peers, how well we can decorate our walls and doors, how we want other teachers to see how we can be better or look better than them, principals hiring friends, teacher putting in a good word to select undeserving teachers for awards, it is about who is most the most qualified and deserving, and who works the hardest to meet the needs of students and sometime, well, all of the time not looking for what they can get out of it. Moreover, what the student can benefit out of the difference you make in their lives every day.

True Grit: *The Best Measure of Success and How to Teach It*

Students learn at different measures. No one can predict whether or not a student will learn their ABC's when they are young, pass his or her test the first time, let alone when or if they will even graduate from high school.

I had a student whom I mentored one year that when I first met them, it would appear to those who judged their outer appearance that they were not smart and would more than likely not graduate from high school. Whereas there was another student who appeared more likely to succeed because their outer appearance seemed more enthusiastic and pleasing to the eye. Well, just to let you know, the student who was judged negatively was the one whose IQ proved to be smarter. They just needed some grit poured into them.

Meeting the needs at every school is important. However, it is more important to meet the needs of the students. And when you have met the needs of the students, you have met the needs of your school building.

They lacked motivation, passion and perseverance for their schoolwork. However, after I began to work with them and helped them get their grades up, encouraged them to come to school to defeat the odds of failure in their life, they began to change their defeated attitude and routine

85

that was not taking them anywhere—skipping school, contemplating dropping out, no drive and no motivation for anything but hanging out in the neighborhood, drugs, and hanging with wrong crowds. All this changed as I showed that student love, passion to help, and a perseverance to not allow them to quit or to give up. You must be this way to each student that enters inside of your school building and classroom. You never know whose life you are touching. You never know what you are working with, and you can never judge a book by its cover because you will most of the time be proven wrong.

Meeting the needs at every school is important. However, it is more important to meet the needs of the students. And when you have met the needs of the students, you have met the needs of your school building. This should be repetitive each day the doors open.

Teaching grit can be quite challenging at times. How you can teach grit in your classroom and in your school is by:

1. Researching what it means.
2. By talking to your students about it.
3. By sharing examples on their level. Elementary school students and middle school students learn on a different level than high school or college students. Examples that are on their level of understanding is important for best results.
4. Share stories of triumph and defeat. Students need to hear about these types of stories so that they will prevent going down that path or giving up hope themselves.
5. Teach the students how to live a gritty lifestyle. Be moderately transparent about your own life's triumphs and failures as it has helped to make you an effective teacher, principle, counselor or coach which will show your students that he or she can do the same with of their own lives.
6. Foster safe environments that encourage grit. Do not be afraid to have fun and share grit in a fun way. You don't want your students to think that learning grit is way too deep or whack.

It is about moving on if there is a mistake made and do not panic or freak out.
7. Help your student practice self-control which has everything to do with grit. For example, if they lose a race or fail a test, it is not the end of the world. They can practice or study harder and try again by racing again or studying harder and pass the test the next time.

What is an Example of Grit?

The greatest example of grit I can provide for you would be learning all of your multiplication cards and having to study hard for about a month just to learn them.

Another great example is that you always have your co-teachers, principals, or student to student's back no matter what. As you lead as a teacher or principal, you have a leader's mindset and a clear goal to work towards each school day. You never allow short-term gains, hectic schedules, or negative feedback to prevent you from continuing to complete all the goals you have set towards the vision for yourself, your students, your classroom, and towards your private life after you leave the school every day. The life that nobody knows but you.

> *As you lead as a teacher or principal, you have a leader's mindset and a clear goal to work towards each school day.*

It is very important to work strenuously toward challenges you may face with each student, in your classroom, in the teacher's lounge, within the leadership team, within the school building, at home, or in a business meeting for business owners. You should maintain an effort and interest despite failure and adversity on your

Stephanie Franklin

school campus as you always remember that it is all about meeting the needs of the students in a gritty way.

Is Grit Really the Key to Success?

Grit is the key to success. It is the paint the painter uses to paint the painting. Without grit, the painting cannot be successfully completed. It is the passion and perseverance that every student, teacher, counselor and administrator need to empower grit in your lives as well as have education or maybe just a goal that seems too hard or impossible to reach.

Grit is the driver of achievement and success made by the teacher, counselor, student, or administrator. The power to persevere is needed to be successful when showing your talents. However, if you really want to do an exceptional job within your talents, you will need perseverance. Without perseverance, your talents are merely unfinished efforts or possibilities.

One year I had a student who felt that dropping out was the best method to solve life issues in her life. Her mother agreed with her decision as she was desperate and determined to give her what she wanted. I heard that she and her mother came to the school to make

> *Grit is the paint the painter uses to paint the painting. Without grit, the painting cannot be successfully completed.*

it official. I walked to the front office and stopped her from walking away with the worst decision of her life.

As we stood in the main hallway, at first it was a struggle to encourage her to stay in school as I continued to let her know that I would help her get her grades up and all her NG's (No grade) off of her record. She had a quick change in heart and agreed. Her mother did as well after a long-drawn-out conversation.

So, the journey began, and it was not an easy one at first but as the year progressed, she began to make a leap of faith and a change in attitude with a persevered will to change everything about herself that she was not happy with. Such as:

1. Obtaining a mindset to bring her grades up.
2. Perseverance to come to school every day instead of on certain days. We are on a block schedule that has certain courses on every other day consisting of A and B-Days. She would always say she did not come to school on A-Days because she did not like her A-Day teachers. However, on B-Days was dressed and ready to show up.
3. Her SEL (Social Emotional Learning) increased greatly and in a positive way as she realized that it was okay to talk to other people in a calm manner that made them feel comfortable, rather in a harsh, loud and over aggressive approach that made them feel uncomfortable about being around her and she around them.

I began to help her by speaking to her teachers on her behalf concerning getting her grades up. I tutored, mentored, counseled, believed in her, helped her to believe in herself, and listened to how she felt. Sometimes we as teachers, principals, counselors, coaches, campus leaders and mentors do not listen enough or long enough to our students and how they feel and what they are going through until after something tragic happens. I helped this student to come from zeros, NG's (no grades), I's (incompletes), negative conduct, beating on walls when she was angry, fighting, and constantly in SAC (In-school suspension and out of school suspension).

It was a process. However, she went from all this to honor roll, some E's in conduct, staying in her classes and not being kicked out for bad behavior. She went from a positive attitude and rapport with her teachers and administrators. I also helped her work on her approach—how she perceived her peers, and how she perceived her teachers and administrators. I helped her change from thinking everybody hated her, and she hated them, along with the hurt of being heavy-set, all the students laughing at her, worrying about what they thought of her, and from lies being told to her. One of her biggest fights were her struggle with the way she felt about catching the bus and her negative conduct when she arrived at school. I'm sure you probably had a student with this same problem. Maybe worse or maybe a bit better. Her insecurities made her think she wasn't good enough as all the other girls made good grades, had promising futures and positive relationships with their teachers, and she didn't.

I share this lengthy but needed story to say that grit—having the passion and perseverance to succeed is what this young lady experienced. Grit is not only for students or people who live positive lives or have positive attitudes; however, grit is for everyone. Grit matters and was successful in this situation as it required pure strength and will for the young lady to make a conscious decision to turn from her negative behavior and lifestyle, to change the way she thought, how she felt about herself and others; and to stay in school and not drop out. She persevered through bad self-esteem and conquered her will to want to give up. I have learned to accept each student differently. They each have their own personalities and hang ups. You cannot treat them all the same and make the good students suffer for the negative students. You help the negative students and praise them all for the good that they all do. I know it sounds crazy to praise negative students, however, I have done this for years and it has worked for me.

The way I successfully do this is by pointing out something good about the student that is showing negative behavior. I also praise by giving him or her a positive alternative in the place of the negative behavior and an incentive when they show good behavior. I have witnessed students who were showing bad behavior change just by doing this. I also remind them of my classroom expectations about getting up without permission and talking without permission. I provide additional accommodations that allows the student to learn on their level of understanding and keep them busy. Every teacher has their own way of reaching the students. However, this is what has worked for me. You may use other ways to reach your students and athletes that may work for you, I say keep doing what works for you.

Many times, teachers see only the surface of the students who show bad behavior but do not realize there are reasons why they are angry, or why they are having temper tantrums or mouthing off to you and the students. We do not know what they face when they go home or leave the school campus each day. So, as the question is asked, is grit really the key to success? I will answer by saying grit is the key to success and is much needed if you want a safe and positive classroom and school environment.

If a student wants to make it through school and graduate, they must exercise grit. If a teacher wants to continue to be successful in the classroom, they must exercise grit. Grit gives power, passion, and perseverance when all odds are against you, when the going gets tough, when unexpected challenges come your way (in school and outside of school), when staff, teachers, and administrators are coming against you for no reason, when unexpected tragedies come up out of nowhere, when the students do not like you, when the students do not want to learn or complete their assignments, when it seems as if you are teaching to an empty classroom but full of students because your students are not listening, when friendships end suddenly, when your job titles play out and is removed out of nowhere, when co-workers stop liking you because you got promoted, when you as a principal feel as though the teachers and staff is not working together and excited about teaching, and so forth.

This reminds me of the Maslow's hierarchy of needs in which categorizes needs as "existence needs, desires for satisfying interpersonal relationships; and growth needs, desires for continued personal growth and development" (Ehiobuche, 2013). This will develop leadership skills and improve campus relatedness and interpersonal relationship needs among the staff. These needs are important to have as it will help the staff to relate to each other as well as the students. As teachers, students and administrators enhance self-esteem, it helps to achieve relatedness needs and growth needs, which in turn affects their performance. In this case, it affected the young lady's drive and performance in a positive way to want to succeed and want to graduate instead of dropping out. I always teach the students to find what they are passionate about. In seeking this step in their lives provides hope to their future and something they can strive for without giving up.

What Are the Five Characteristics of Grit? How Many Can You List?

In order to give you five characteristics of grit, you must first know what the characteristics of grit mean. The characteristic of grit means to identify someone with grit. Duckworth, (2015) mentions, they are courage, conscientiousness, long-term goal oriented, resilience, and excellence (Duckworth, (2015).

Another way of listing them in my own way as I have had experience working with these types of students and people who would show bravery to win, reliable—can be counted on, endurance, quality and brilliance; and completion and tweak—fix what may not have worked right away but was eventually completed.

> **Bravery to win— Ex: turning each assignment in on time even when you've had trouble.**

Having the characteristics of grit is showing courage and strength of character to exemplify an irrepressible personality, or that will not back down in the face of obstacles or failures. For example, a student with ADHD attempting to read a complete sentence who quickly gave up after not being able to pronounce the harder words within the sentence, so they quickly gave up after the first try.

What are examples of grit?

1. An athlete who is mentally tough and are more consistent than others. They are not late to practice. They don't miss workouts.
2. A writer, an artist, and an employee who is mentally tough and delivers on a more consistent basis than most.
3. A leader that is mentally tough and are more consistent than their peers. They have a clear short-term goal that they work towards each day to accomplish.

5 Characteristics of Grit—

1. Bravery to win—*Ex: turning each assignment in on time even when you've had trouble.*
2. Reliable—*gets the job done quickly and completes all assignments on-time.*
3. Endurance—*setting short-term and long-term goals and completing them.*
4. Quality and brilliance—*providing excellent well thought out work.*
5. Completion and tweak (if necessary).

How Many Characteristics Can You List? *Name them and name them in detail.*
1.
2.
3.
4.
5.

Embrace Social & Emotional Learning with Grit

- Why is Social Emotional Learning Needed in the School District?
- Using Social & Emotional Learning with Grit
- How to Use Grit in mentorship and Social Emotional Learning
- Controlling Your Actions
- Success Comes with The Best
- Build a Culture of Collaboration
- Why Practice Self-Awareness in the Classroom?

There is much more to understand and articulate about developing grit in our youth today. Grit goes beyond the classroom, in fact, it does not just pop up out of the invisible world. It requires teaching the children and youth to be leaders who cultivates passion, strength, perseverance, provides a path to a successful career choice, and creates opportunities. One way of doing this is through Social-Emotional Learning (SEL) interventions and learning that falls in the category of grit. It is the process through which children, youth and adults acquire and effectively apply the knowledge, attitudes and skills necessary to understand and manage emotions; set and achieve positive goals; feel and show empathy for others; establish and maintain positive relationships; and make responsible decisions.

> *Each student should be embraced and told that they each can do anything but fail. They each must be told to love one another no matter the color, gender, age or creed.*

The SEL definition comes from CASEL, which stands for the Collaborative for Academic, Social, and Emotional Learning (CASEL). It is a skill often associated with grit that is connected to five of the core SEL competencies such as, courage, conscientiousness, perseverance, resilience, and passion. CASEL is the leading national organization dedicated to advance the science, practice and policy of SEL. This is the "building block" to helping students excel socially, emotionally, and in a meaningful way.

This chapter is dear to my heart as the world has made a complete 360 degree turn for the worse. With the Corona virus—Covid-19, from George Floyd to all of the lives that have been affected by police brutality to a bittersweet way of life as the virus has caused the United States to change to a new way normal—virtual and shelter in place to stay at home with family and family time—bringing families close and/or closer together. As an educator, coach and mentor, it is important for me to teach all students whether Caucasian, African American, Hispanic, Latino, African, Chinese, Vietnamese and so on how to respect one another, the value in it and appreciate where each other come from—building a climate culture is the key.

Why is Social Emotional Learning with Grit Needed in the School District?

Social & Emotional Learning with Grit is terribly needed within each school district as well as on every school campus; not to mention every school classroom. Each teacher and principal, during this time whether physically or virtually must teach by adding this subject within your class instruction or school's vision. Every student, no matter the color, gender or creed must be told that they are somebody. They must be told that they each are valued, and they should embrace the integrity of their race and culture without being laughed at, belittled, treated with disrespect, attacked with prejudice remarks, bringing up those that are of the same race or gender and tearing down those that are not. Also, provoking those students to anger you know you can get in trouble and then when they take the bait, you give them SAC (In-School Suspension), OSS (Out of School Suspension) or send them off to alternative schools. Last but certainly not least, teacher and administrator bullying—bullying students and raising up impossible expectations that you know they cannot meet. Students learn best when teachers and administrators show no biasness and showing concern and being nice to them.

SEL is needed within each grade level in several ways.

I will list some conflict examples of how SEL is needed and provide a solution:

1. **First Graders-** Name calling and cutting in line.
2. **Second Graders-** Stealing someone's milk cartridge or pulling someone's hair for no reason.
3. **Third-Fifth Graders-** Name Calling on social media, passing notes while the teacher is teaching, and pushing in the lunch line.
4. **Six- Eight Graders-** Clicks, talking back to the teacher, disrespecting authority, calling the principal out his or her name, contraband found in lockers and on students after search or repeated district dress code violations. Negative social media, sexting (texting nude photos and texting posting them online) and sex trafficking in the community.
5. **Ninth-Twelfth Graders-** Illegal cell phone usage, gang fights, and social media brawls. Illegal use of narcotics, contraband found in lockers and on students after search, the sharing of pills on the campus and sex trafficking in the community. Clicks, talking back to the teacher, hitting the teacher or staff, disrespecting authority, and calling the principal out his or her name. District and campus-wide dress code violations, etc. etc. etc. And the list goes on and on.

Solution 1 to the conflict examples- on each grade level as you embrace SEL on your campus (1st-4th grade)- is by allowing incentives for students who share with each other, or they put the glue back where it belongs without being told to or pick up the toys in the play area without being told to.

Solution 2 to the conflict examples- Another solution to these conflicts on your campus (5th-12th grade)- is by setting up a community circle on your campus where students can come together, build a positive relationship and talk freely about the problems they each are facing whether on their campus, in the classroom or in their neighborhood and community. I have had the opportunity to help many students in this area whether in my classroom or within my mentor program who just needed to vent. Most times students, no matter first grade all the way up to twelfth grade just need someone to talk to when negative behavior is prevalent. After they vent, they become a whole new person and their conduct and academics reflect it.

By creating a community circle, you are bridging the gap and creating a positive campus culture and climate for learning. I have used the community circle, sometimes I call it the hurt circle, as I allow each student to vent about things that are on their minds that bother them or just want somebody to talk to. I found that peer grouping is the best way to get the best out of students because youth beget youth as students beget students. Sometimes students feel that nobody understands them but their peers. So, this was and still is very successful for my mentoring sessions and interventions. I know you may be asking why didn't I add a separate conflict solution for the 5th-8th graders? Why did I add 5th-12th graders all together? Well, I will answer as they each have the same problems and emotional outburst. They each share the same conflicts on each campus whether it is middle school or high school. The student's negative behavior is pretty much the same. So, the method I have used with my mentees have been successful. I've had to search for many different interventions that would work for the students on my campus, just about all of them I've thought of myself, however, I can say that majority, to all, have been successful.

Each campus is different and will require you to seek what actually works for your campus and campus vision. You and your leadership team (if applies to you) must research and apply professional developments and RTI (Response to Intervention) interventions that will work for your campus, staff and students that will be beneficial to meet the needs of all of your students and staff. The ultimate goal is to meet the needs of ALL students and their academic, emotional, social and safety learning and success.

Nothing else matters. It is not about who can come up with the best intervention, or who wants to be heard or give their idea just to say that they have added a response, it is <u>ONLY</u> about implementing what will work for your campus and meet the needs of all students. Too many campuses are meeting the needs of themselves rather than the needs of the students. Their concern is on how to make the school look good rather than meeting the needs of the students. This should not be the goal of the campus vision nor the vision of each teacher, staff, assistant principal, nor the presiding building principal. The goal is to teach, inform and motivate each student to follow school and district guidelines and procedures to be successful in each class and instruction, and see to the needs of each student's social and emotional learning prosper. If we stick to the basics and not try to be like other campuses because of what they are doing may not work for your campus. Stick to the basics of what is working for your campus.

As I have researched the internet and I have noticed that more and more school districts are turning towards SEL as a focus strategy to improve school culture and climate, student engagement, and improving student learning.

Each student should be embraced and be told that they each can do anything but fail. They each must be told to love one another no matter the color, gender, age or creed. We fail as parents, teachers, administrators, principals and community leaders when we allow students to come to our schools, inside of our classrooms, homes or communities and treat each other unkind because of the color of our skin and not address it but agree with it. This should not be so. The true fact is that since you may have been raised by your parents to dislike African Americans, Hispanics, Caucasians, Chinese or any other race, and when you birthed children, you taught them to do the same. This should not be so. This passes from generation down to generation. However, the key is love and respect bottom line.

Change must come within our school districts, schools, and classrooms. The change begins within you. Social & Emotional Learning with Grit focuses on understanding each student who falls within this category. Most people attempt to judge this area as only the troublemakers are at-risk students or students who have mental issues and are not capable of being alone. This is a statistic that is just not true. There are all kinds of different social and emotional students who are very smart with a high GPA (Grade Point Average) but struggle with emotional and social skills. I have mentored some of these types of students. You cannot afford to judge the outer appearance; however, the inner is what needs to be evaluated and addressed. There are many school districts that are lacking in this area. There is no perfect answer to this subject, however, there is a workable and successful solution to this problem. LOVE and COMPASSION show no bias answers when it comes to working with these types of behaviors no matter the race or gender.

Using Social & Emotional Learning with Grit

We must exemplify each student in such a way that they each demonstrate love, respect for each other, and endure with them even when their behavior is negative and positive change is nowhere in the horizon. When good behavior, lack of motivation to learn, and a positive attitude is nowhere to be seen. Those are the ones we work harder to reach, encourage and to love. I have experienced this with my students as well as with my mentees within my Mentor Program, "The Winning Team," as at times I struggled to reach them when it seemed as if some would never change. However, with grit—I had and have LOVE and COMPASSION to help them and persevering with them to see change. I have encouraged them even when everyone else gave up on them. I endured with them until I seen or see change; and met the individual need socially, emotionally, and academically; as I have had the opportunity to complete these many goals and still do to this day. We must let our youth—African Americans, Caucasians, Hispanics, Chinese, Vietnamese, Latinos, Africans, Indians, etc. believe in themselves and that they each can accomplish any goal that is set before them.

How to Use Grit in Mentorship and Social Emotional Learning

I can recall a student I had that from the outside had a tall 350, rough looking appearance. Everybody was intimidated by his presence and behavior. One day he came to my classroom and stated that his friend told him good things about me and my mentor program and how I help students with bad behavior and bad grades. He stated that he wanted help and was ready to change his negative ways. The first words that came out of my mouth was, "I appreciate you coming to my class and believing in my help as I help others but are you really ready to change?"

He quickly answered, "yes mam'."

I immediately began to help him by dealing with his social and emotional challenges as well as negative behavior and counseled against his will to drop out. Now mind you, it did not happen overnight, it was a process, but with these steps below, it finally happened little by little. The reward was that his grades were brought up to passing and later on brought up to AB honor roll. His negative behavior made a 360 degree turn in a positive way. I taught him in a gritty way to have integrity, confidence, and perseverance within himself even when he made mistakes and did not change right away. I taught him the value of respecting other students, girls and teachers even when he didn't agree with them. I taught him to respect administrators. I also taught him to see the importance of getting a high school diploma and encouraged him to believe in himself and to know that he was smart, and that all he had to do was to come to school not for the teachers he did not like, but for himself. So, he did just that and his life was changed.

He began to come to school everyday. He stopped fighting and started going to class and being on time. He brought his grades up to passing and on up to AB honor roll. He passed on to the next grade level when before he came to me it was not going to happen. Again, it was a process to help change him. It did not happen overnight although I have helped some to do that. However, in his case, it was a process. I encourage every mentor, teacher, coach, and principal trying to do what I am doing to take it one day at a time and do not rush students to learn nor rush students who fall short in the area of SEL to change overnight. As you follow each point below, every school day or every time your mentoring doors open, it will get easier, and they will change. Your help must be from your heart and not from your paycheck. You cannot successfully win with a youth group, children or students while trying to help them for money, or for a stipend or a higher salary. You MUST do it with a willing heart and a compassion to want to help them and to see them changed for the better, and to be successful across the board whether academically, emotionally, and physically. It may not work for all of them as we realize we cannot reach all of them, however, we strive to reach as many as we can, no matter the cost.

1. I used the grit technique by showing passion and compassion to want to help and believe in the student. *(also, with others—male and female)*
2. I built a lasting positive relationship with the student with trust and hope filled. *(also, with others—male and female)*

3. I used the grit technique by persevering with the student when he did not change right away. *(also, with others—male and female)*
4. I encouraged the student to believe in himself and to have confidence to want to make good grades rather than accept barely passing or defeat. These steps also apply to the countless of young ladies I have had and have the opportunity to help each year as well.
5. Leadership matters within our schools and classes for all students. There is no child or youth that should be left behind. I helped this student and others—male and female by building character and increase this student's comprehension and knowledge by tutoring and after school mentorship program on a daily to weekly basis.

Controlling Your Actions

Each student, teacher, staff, administrator, and principal should control their actions as your actions have consequences. Each of us are held responsible and accountable for everything we do against someone else *(this applies to staff, co-workers, and students)* and what we say against someone else, especially in a way that would provoke anger within someone else that would provoke them to retaliate. Many times, teachers, staff, administrators, and principals think they are in the clear from doing wrong or being guilty because of the position they uphold, when in fact they are capable of being more wrong than the student. This is why every situation must be evaluated by whoever is guilty and must be dealt with accordingly. You are just as responsible as the students are—whoever is wrong for their actions. No one is exempt from doing wrong to another human being.

There are some that are very sneaky in so that they provoke but can't deal with the backlash of the offender (the one they offended). Once that person gets offended, they lash back with provoked anger and fight back. The one who started it can't deal with it so they fight when the fight could have been avoided if the one who started it would have controlled their anger in the first place.

So, what we need to do now is we need to deal with the root so that the anger can be destroyed. If we destroy the root, the rest of the root (vines) is going to be destroyed as well. Such as, bad attitudes, anger, in-school suspension, SAC time, detention, dropout rates, jail time, or even death on arrival. On the teacher and administrator side: when the root is destroyed, it will destroy proud attitudes of nobody is a better teacher than me, nobody is a better administrator or even a better principal than me. Here is another root: students will always be wrong in my eyesight, and I will never admit that I am wrong because of the position I uphold. I can yell at innocent students because it doesn't matter how they feel. I don't yell at Tommy because he has a better upbringing, Bella doesn't know English good so I will not place her with other English-speaking students so she won't pull them down, I can add points to a Caucasian student before a Hispanic student or even an African American student's grade and it's okay in my eyesight. As a principal I can hire or remove a teacher or staff out of a position because I want to hire or put in my best friend or the one I like rather than the one who is most qualified. As an assistant principal, I can send bad students off to alternative schools even though they are innocent and have done no wrong, but because of their reputation, how gangster they look, and background I can do this because of the position I uphold. No one will find out and I will get away with it. All of these roots must be uprooted, dealt with and destroyed in order to have a successful district, school campus, and classroom.

It is all about growth mindset and using gritty in ways to change their passion to fight and disrupt to have a passion for the other person to respect them even when you do not agree with them. It is also about persevering with them when times get rough and working out the conflict instead of creating the conflict. Most times this is what escalates into detrimental outcomes. If children and youth know what you fear, and that you are afraid of them, you are the easiest to control. I encourage teachers, staff, administrators, and principals not to be afraid of students, especially when they are over aggressive and when they are not your race or from your culture. Grit is having passion for everybody.

This same method applies to parents/guardians and their children as well. During the Corona Covad-19 virus, when everyone was instructed to stay in their homes and practice social distancing, parents/guardians were forced to teach their children virtually and physically. This was an over whelming change that caused households all over the world to change. No one is exempt from showing grit to all children, students, and to one another—having passion toward one another and persevering to complete this important goal.

As a parent you cannot neglect to help your child when they need help. It cannot be all on the teacher, administrator, community or stakeholder to raise students. It takes a village and all hands-on deck to help meet the needs of all students. All hands in connecting with one another. All hands uniting with one another. All hands getting down to the nitty *gritty* at all times to meet the needs of students and staff in-so-that we all are successful every school day and every year. Success comes when there is no division. Success comes when student's educational needs are met.

Success Comes with The Best—*Levers Are Important*
In order to have a successful campus with at-risk students, the district must hire the best teachers that fit that position. Many times, districts are not doing their research in hiring the best teachers. They are hiring to fill a position rather than select the well qualified. I understand that it is hard to fill positions when working with at-risk students. They are strong willed in their behavior and in what they do and in wanting their way, so there needs to be a strong mentor or

teacher leader who can handle this area. The week qualified for that position.

Levers are used to identify and describe talent management that can be used on your campus and with your team of teachers and administrators. These levers are used to improve teaching teams and reach its goals; and use teachers who share the school and community's core values. Your goal as a principal and school should be to bring teachers on-board who are deeply committed to the mission of your school campus, reflective teachers and administrators, and hardworking. Questions you should ask is, "Are they for kids? Do they love students who are not of the same race? Are they hard working? Are they collaborative? Are they a TEAM player? Do they TEAM their talents up with other teachers, parents, and stakeholders? What is their commitment level to your campus vision? What is their grit level on your campus, with students, and the classroom? Do they have the same goals as your school-wide mission and vision?

In order to help make this happen, using these key levers below on your campus will bring success as you look to meet academic needs of your students and teachers.

Study the charts below:

LEVER- 1 RECRUITMENT AND ON-BOARD ACTIONS	**Action 1: Recruitment-** Identify effective and aligned staff candidates. **Action 2: Selection and Hiring-** Implement Rigorous screening and hiring process. **Action 3: Staff Assignment-** Implement processes for strategic staff assignments.

	Action 4: Induction- Develop systems to introduce new staff to school expectations, processes, and procedures.
LEVER 2- INSTRUCTIONAL LEADERSHIP TEAM ACTIONS	**Action 1: Instructional Leadership** Team Roles, Expectations and Support- Identify, develop, and support instructional leadership team members. **Action 2: Teacher Leadership-** Create on-going opportunities for teachers to build leadership compacity.
LEVER 3- PERFORMANCE MONITORING AND EVALUATION	**School Leaders** monitor and manage staff performance by providing regular, accurate feedback. **Action 1: Performance and Expectations-** Set expectations for all staff members that define what standards and actions will be accessed.

	Action 2: Observation and Actionable Feedback- Gather evidence of practice through frequent observations and provide concrete feedback. **Action 3: Monitoring Implementation-** Assess where changes are occurring and where additional supports are needed. **Action 4: Performance Evaluation-** At the end of the year, review all evidence to access individual performance.
LEVER 4: PROFESSIONAL LEARNING AND COLLABORATION	The most powerful learning happens inside of school is directly connected to what's happening in classrooms. **Action 1: Ongoing Professional Learning-** Provide job-embedded opportunities to learn and practice new skills.

	Action 2: Collaborative teacher team structures- Establish structures that facilitate collaborative teacher planning and learning.

The chart above is very important in terms of having a well-qualified teacher in place to work with at-risk and RTI students. There is no way students can excel without you as a leader. The school cannot be great without your leadership. It takes a TEAM to win a game. There are no I's in TEAM.

Do your best to relate to all students no matter their race, background or culture. Look for ways to build staffing and professional learning in these areas. Build capacity with teacher leaders and foster a culture of collaboration in strategic steps.

Build a Culture of Collaboration

It is important to build culture and collaboration on your campus. How do you accomplish this? You accomplish this by first, believing in your staff, teachers and administrators. I have learned that people will give you more when you believe in them. And it is not by only offering them free fully loaded baked potatoes during their lunch time in your teacher's lounge. Or free pop cycles as they are leaving for the day. It is about believing in their gifts and educational talents that they each can bring to the table. This is where building a culture for collaboration takes position. Building a team of teacher leaders who help make decisions on how to build student morale, teacher morale and culture based on the type of students and teachers you have on your campus.

Every campus is different. You must not, as they say, keep up with the Jone's. This is an old saying but a true one. What this means is you cannot keep up with other school campuses. You cannot look at a school that is better off than yours at the moment or copy what they are doing. You must build what you have in the position of where your campus is or where your students are. One will say do not be inspired by other campuses, however I say, it is okay to be inspired, just do not put your campus and staff in a position of trying to copy them and their success in areas where your campus is struggling, and it is too much for your them to handle; and it would take a miracle to do what they are doing. Take one day at a time and do only what you can do and what your campus can handle.

Why Practice Self-Awareness in the Classroom?
- By acknowledging your own emotions, and how your emotions may play into your reactions.
- Explicitly name the skills you are using as you model them.
- View students as collaborators in developing social-emotional skills like coping skills, setting goals, and getting along with others.

Practicing self-awareness is important as we explore further and find out more about ERG theory. It is the development of Maslow's hierarchy of needs that categories needs as, "existence needs, desires for satisfying interpersonal relationships; and growth needs, desires for continued personal growth and development" (Ehiobuche, 2013). This alone will develop and improve interpersonal relationships among teachers and staff and campus readiness. Maslow's hierarchy of needs are important as they relate and help the teachers, staff and students to relate to one another. The enhancement of self-esteem among the teachers, staff and students helps with achieving relatedness needs and growth needs, which affect their performance. When social emotional learning is embraced, this is when cultural proficiency develops, in which is about serving the needs of all students, with a laser-like focus on historically underserved students. When education is offered in a culturally proficient manner, historically underserved students gain access to educational opportunities intended to result in high academic achievement.

How Grit Applies to RTI (Response to Intervention)

RTI (Response to Intervention), is an assessment tool aimed at early identification of children with learning issues. Students who receive rigorous, effective interventions early on are most likely to succeed through RTI. With grit, they have the passion and perseverance to press through the stress and struggle to succeed and overcome their difficulties.

Within this process, students who show signs of learning difficulties are provided with a sequence of increasingly intensive and personalized instruction. This intervention process is designed and presented by an educational staff in collaboration with special educators and school psychologists and includes systematic monitoring of the student's progress. If a child does not respond to instruction or a series of interventions—RTI, that child is considered to have a learning disability and may be in need of Special Education services.

One day I gave my students a challenging assignment that caused them to think the assignment through in-so-that they each had to literally work together. They worked endlessly to complete the assignment and was almost unsuccessful until I mentioned that if

"Stress is a choice."
...How do we handle stress and struggle?

117

they conquer the assignment successfully and all together, I will buy the entire class donuts. The very moment I mentioned the word "donuts," their eyes lit up like light bulbs as they all clapped and cheered. I asked them the question, "why are you all so excited about donuts?"

Several of them answered, "because we ain't never had no donuts before."

I couldn't believe what I heard. This taught me to never take my life and the freedom of choice for granted. Donuts were nothing to me. They were just donuts that I could get anytime I had a taste for them. However, it was quite different with these students. Most of them have hard lives and challenging environments and we as educators, staff and administrators should never take them for granted, nor should we take our own individual lives for granted.

How does this apply to you as a single individual, or a mother, a father, a teacher, a coach, an assistant principal, a principal, or even a superintendent over a school district? Write your thoughts below and share them with others if you want:

_____
_____
_____
_____
_____
_____
_____
_____
_____
_____
_____
_____
_____
_____
_____
_____

There was a time as an educator I had to endure coming to school and teach classes after the passing of my mother. She was my best friend and sister. It was very hard to persevere, however, I remembered that if I quit, I would be quitting on her and all of my students who mean so much to me; and their success was and still is important to me. My mother would want me to carry on and enjoy my life and not worry about things that I could not change. Just when things got a little better they got worse. My father passed away months after my mom. The load was much too great. So, David Zerfoss, (2011) words stuck in my brain—don't worry about the small stuff. The small stuff will take care of themselves, live for today as tomorrow will take care of itself. Enjoy yourself, spouse, children (if any), family, and dear friends while you have them and do not take your lives for granted.

We as educators and administrators spend most of our time, day, and effort to help every student that comes our way, that we neglect family, friends, and your "me" time. There must be a balance. Although there is a great need in this RTI area, there is a greater need to take care of yourself so that you can continue to be successful in this area.

As we move deeper into this chapter, the question is asked: how does grit apply to RTI? As RTI is a process used by educators to help students who may be struggling with their negative behavior, or a lesson they do not understand, or skill they're having a hard time conquering, the teacher will use interventions, such as, behavior interventions or teaching procedures in order to help the struggling student or students succeed in the classroom. This is where grit comes in the picture, it works through interventions, where students are able to obtain power, passion, and perseverance to work through their struggles only to know that they each can overcome them. For example, they can overcome a math problem they are having trouble with. Or what about when a student is lacking self confidence in an English class and has to persevere to believe in themselves? Or even an engineering student who is studying robotics and having to code the robot in order to make it move, or having trouble reading the ruler in order to use measurements properly and successfully in order to build the robot?

What is RTI (Response to Intervention)?

Response to Intervention (RTI) is a multi-tier approach to the early identification and support of students with learning and behavior needs. Struggling learners are provided with interventions at increasing levels of intensity to accelerate their rate of learning. As I mentor my mentees, learning behavior needs have risen on the subjects of fighting, drugs, pill popping, and mobility rates—not having enough and stealing to fulfill the need is what most would say. Or "I get high so I don't have to worry about my problems." As these truthful examples are stated, there is a stronghold to increase learning and accelerate social and emotional interventions, and academic curriculum and success.

We must provide successful interventions that cater to all students' needs, not only academic needs for students or students who do not struggle in this area. Most times, by experience, if you cater to the social emotional level within each student or child, there will be an increase and acceleration within their academics and conduct. I have witnessed this. When this area is neglected, you can rest assure there will be negative behavior, drawbacks, and withdrawal issues until this area is successfully addressed and dealt

The Power of Grit in the Classroom, School, and Community

with. This is where the three tiers come in. Refer to the next page for your reference.

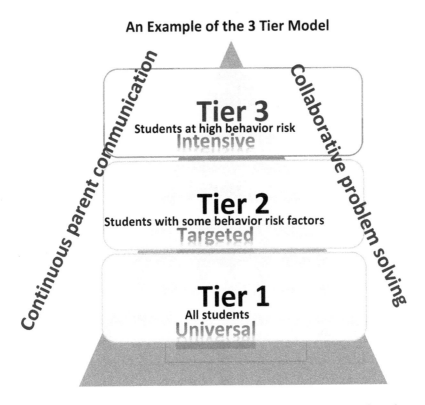

An Example of the 3 Tier Model in <u>Your School</u>

What Does Your School's 3 Tier Model Look Like?

Write it on the blanks on the next page.

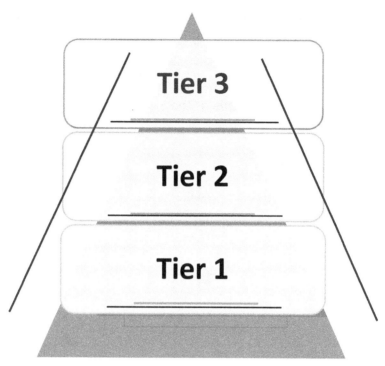

Name of Your School _____

School Year _____

% of Students at School Are At-Risk Students _____

Number of Students at the School _____

Is RTI (Response to Intervention) Effective?

There is a strict common implementation to RTI. When identifying a student for Tier 2, along with a standard set of interventions, there is a significantly negative effect for RTI interventions. Changing tier to tier, involves early identification of students' learning problems and the use of focused lessons, or interventions that are usually more-intensive "tiers" of instruction—to improve learning (Education Week, (2015). Tier 1 students receive consistent instruction in a chosen subject along with ongoing problems that may emerge.

RTI For Diverse Learners

Students must overcome culture shock that holds them back from being a diverse learner. The question and challenge is, are the teachers teaching these students? Most teachers find the challenge harder than most as they seek to find ways and instructional interventions that cater to the success of these students whose backgrounds, living status, home cultures and status', languages, and other cases that are different than their own.

Most teachers are not ready to deal with or to respond to these diverse areas within students. This is particularly true in ELL (English Language Learners) with behavior and learning problems that have increased within schools and school districts all across the globe in the area of reading and differences in language. We as a village (parents, mentors, coaches, educators, counselors, assistant principals, principals, board members, superintendents, stakeholders, and spiritual guides) have got to find a way to help these students and that will cater to their needs so that they all can be successful learners everyday. Sadly, the issues that causes and maintains the achievement gap exists between dominant culture and minority students.

How TTESS *(Texas Teacher Evaluation & Support System)* Applies to Grit

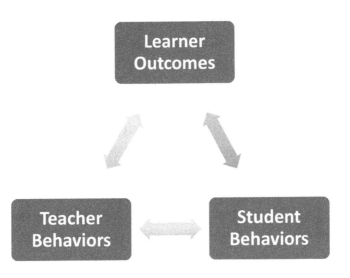

The T-TESS Triangle: Evaluation Focus

T-TESS strives to bridge the gap between teachers and students and the effectiveness of teaching in a consistent way. It focuses on how students react to the teacher's instructional practices.

The *Learner Outcomes* refer to the TEKS and/or other standards that identify the focus outcome of the lesson (Pre-K Guidelines, ELPS, TA TEKS, etc.). The appraiser listens for the Learner Outcomes or the lesson objectives as the anchorman of the appraiser. You, as the teacher, should prepare for these points and answer these questions before you are appraised by your appraiser:

1. What are the outcomes of your lesson?
2. How are they consistently and consecutively communicated to students?
3. What evidence is there to support to show that your students understood the lesson?
4. How does evidence reflect that student's understood and mastered the learner outcomes?

The *Student Behavior* allows the appraiser to collect evidence regarding what students do (interact/collaborate) and say (audio) throughout the lesson as they each use the learner outcome as a filter for how they each respond and behave to classroom instruction. Evidence would determine whether or not students met the learner outcomes. The appraiser is informed about aspects of the lesson, such as, where the class is in terms of the unit of study—at the beginning, middle, or at the end of the unit to gather relevant information for the pre-conference, lesson plan, etc. If there is any struggle in regard to this effort, perseverance and the passion to gather evidence in spite of would result in grit. Rather than leave and give up, the appraiser is determined to gather evidence for learner outcomes regardless.

The *Teacher Behavior* consist of the appraiser collecting evidence regarding the teacher's behavior and how they are aligned to support the mastery of the identified learner outcomes.

Some questions to consider:

- What is the teacher doing and saying that aligns with and supports the learning objectives? For example: How is the lesson structured to facilitate the student's mastery towards the learner outcomes?

- How does technology, questions, etc., align with the learner outcomes?

It is important to provide evidence for a teacher's behavior in relation to a student's behavior as a connection to the educational relationship.

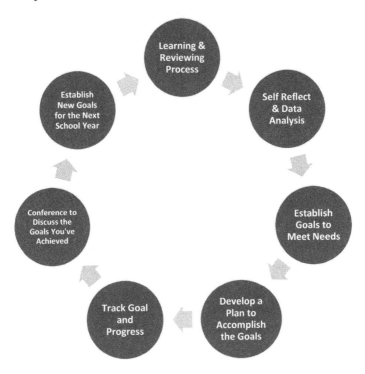

T-TESS Involves These Components:

- A professional development plan and continual goal setting.
- The evaluation cycle, such as, observations, pre conferences and post conferences.

Grit can apply to anyone, anything and any situation that requires a person to have a passion to persevere through anything that will help them to be successful in the classroom, school and in life. The Texas Teacher Evaluation and Support System (T-TESS) is a system that is designed by educators to support teachers in their professional growth, which can mean any areas they may need attention to help them in their success as a teacher. For example, planning, classroom instruction, learning environment, and professional practices and responsibilities.

T-TESS has a positive aspect as the appraisal process helps develop collaboration and dialogue between the appraiser and the teacher. Each teacher must be appraised each year. The appraisal is based on the teacher's performance within their teaching assignments where they are certified.

As it is important for educators to continuously improve their educational practices through professional development, it causes teachers to improve their classroom instruction and causes administrators to become better school and district leaders.

T-TESS is great in a gritty way as it provides effective professional development and enables educators to develop the skills and knowledge they each need to address students' learning challenges even at times when some students may be struggling or feel challenged in a way that they are not learning in a particular subject. Teachers persevere to reach their goals for the success of the student through those times of difficulty and uncertainty and provide interventions and interactions that provide high-quality learning experiences to all students (children and youth).

The Grit Characteristic Check
How Many Do You have?

We can identify the characteristics of grit with five points that sums it up. Below I have added what those characteristics are:

1. **Courage.** When a student, teacher or administrator thinks of courage in the school or classroom, they think of having the courage to complete a task when all of the odds are against them. Courage with grit is a student using bravery to complete an assignment that they did not understand. A teacher assigning an assignment that they had trouble preparing. An administrator using mechanisms that they are not confident will work with the students, teachers or staff.

   The characteristics of grit are courage, perseverance, resilience, passion, and conscientiousness.

2. **Perseverance.** Ability to persevere when you cannot see the successful outcome.
3. **Resilience.** Having the strength to complete a homework assignment that seems impossible to complete. Having the toughness as a teacher to assign an assignment that the

students dread doing. Having the flexibility as an administrator to allow the students to choose which lunch line they would like to stand in rather choosing for them.
4. **Passion.** Having the passion to complete a task (homework assignment, class assignment, tutoring assignment, after school activity task, and/or athletic workout) and love doing it.
5. **Conscientiousness.** It is the ability of achievement oriented—exemplifying a drive to achieve verses someone being dependable—ability to be counted on. It is excellence versus perfection. Conscientiousness is the trait of being careful, vigilant or thorough.

I use these characteristics in my classroom and within my mentor program. The one that really sticks out is resilience. Resilience has been the most needed during time of the pandemic. Everyone has needed strength as teachers need it to take care of things at home, take COVID precautions to wear a mask and stay safe from the virus, give virtual and face-to-face assignments, and teachers and administrators the strength to control bad behavior and students not wanting to complete assignments because of the lack of resilience and motivation.

While mentoring my students, the first thing they all say is, when they had to stay at home all of the time and there was nowhere to go. You may say what does this have to do with them completing assignments? I will say it has a lot to do with it. They've lost their motivation and reliance to keep pushing. My mentoring techniques and sessions helps to increase in a positive way in this area. Toughness pertains to resilience. It is having the capacity to recover quickly from difficulties, either in their homes, in their lives, in their neighborhoods or at school.

A particular person surrenders themselves to life's ups and downs to adjust their goals and attitudes according to the depth of the situation they may encounter. Resilient people also tend to have a strong moral compass or set of beliefs that cannot be shattered.

How Many Characteristics Do I Have? My Sample.

In my classroom

Courage, resilience, perseverance, conscientiousness, and passion.

In my school

Resilience, perseverance, conscientiousness, and passion.

In my spare time

Perseverance and conscientiousness.

In my home

Perseverance, conscientiousness, passion.

With my kids

Courage, resilience, perseverance, conscientiousness, and passion.

How Many Characteristics Do <u>You</u> Have? Please explain.

In my classroom

In my school

In my spare time

In my home

With my kids

How Can I Help My Child Develop Grit?

There are 4 stages to helping your child develop grit within their lives, school, and daily interests.

1. **Passion.** Help them or him or her find their passion—what they love to do. Help them follow what interest them the most. Developing interests is important than mentioning to them their weakness.

2. **Practice.** Help your child find and complete short term and long-term goals. Help them focus 100% on their goals and you may even strive to complete the short term and long-term goals with them. You may also want to get feedback from them on how the progress is going. Lastly, help them finetune their passion/skill if necessary. They may even accomplish their short term and long-term goal(s) the first time.

   > *Developing interests is important than mentioning to them their weakness.*

3. **Purpose.** We all have a purpose in life, and this is valuable. Your child's purpose in life is valuable. It is important to value your child's purpose no matter if you do not agree with it. Let them follow their own dreams. You can guide

them as they pursue them, however, do not control who and what they want to become. It will save you a whole lot of heartaches, headaches and disconnections with your children. Grit helps your child to follow their purpose as they persevere and endure not to give up until they see their purpose come to past. They may have some challenges and hard times as they pursue their purpose and dreams. However, through grit, your help and guidance will help them not give up.

4. **Hope.** Create a sense of hope in your children by believing in them. Too many parents are so wrapped up in work, traveling (work or personal), and/or hanging with friends rather than supporting and believing in their children. Too many times we hear of children hanging with wrong crowds and friendships that mean them no good. It is important to believe in them even when they do not believe in themselves. Your words are valuable to them, and they do listen to every word you say even when it does not seem like they do.

5. **Perseverance.** Perseverance is a word that provides all of these: persistence, tenacity, dedication, determination and diligence. There are times when your child may be frustrated or lost in who they are, lost in making the right decisions, lost in picking the right friends, lost with determining who's for them and who's not, lost in how to study for a test they do not understand, lost on what job to take, or what career to go into, or what sport to pursue, how to get better in the academic or sporting activities they are involved in each day, this is when grit shows up in you as the parent— persistence, tenacity, dedication, determination and diligence , love and encouragement to help them get through them and be successful.

Below write down how you plan to help your child develop grit.

Your Plan	Mon	Tues	Wed
Goal(s)			
Purpose			
Did you complete it?			
How do you feel completing it?			
Classwork			
Chores around the house			

Thurs	Fri	Sat	Sun

Jot down your plan(s) in more detail below.

_____
_____
_____
_____
_____
_____
_____
_____

Stephanie Franklin

Positive feedback is important if you want your child to listen to you. Feeding them with negativity—always speaking down on them, telling them what they cannot do, rather than what they can do will develop low self-esteem, they will look down on themselves and others (at school, at home, everywhere they go), they will show a lack of grit—no persistence, no tenacity, no dedication, no determination, no diligence, low grades or failing grades with no hope to pull them up, don't want to wake up and stays in bed all day, no drive to complete their assignments at school, no drive to complete their chores at home, talking back to you as the parent and authorities, leaving and staying out all night after you have given them a curfew, threatening words of suicide, and so much more.

Being that grit is having passion and the power to persevere through anything, as you are the parent, your child is depending on you to help them, and this is why positive feedback is very important even when they may work your last nerve at times. You must set a goal and follow through to complete it to talk positive when spending time with your children, whether they are young or adults. You must give positive feedback when sharing quality time or when they are confused and need your guidance.

On the chart below, I would like for you to add how you are going to be positive, speak positive and give positive feedback toward your child in a gritty way.

Your Positive Approach	Mon	Tues	Wed
The way you talk to them			
Their accomplishments			
With helping them			
With School Work			
With their self-esteem			
Chores around the house			
When they smart off at you			
When they choose a career you're not happy with			

Your Positive Approach	Thurs	Fri	Sat	Sun
The way you talk to them				
Their accomplishments				
With helping them				
With School Work				
With their self-esteem				
Chores around the house				
When they smart off at you				
When they choose a career you're not happy with				

How Do You Raise a Gritty Child?

Raising a gritty child is not always the easiest thing to do. You must be very patient and cheer them on through every obstacle and every step of the way. Children and youth are not fully mature as adults are, so they need special attention, love and the assurance that someone loves and cares about them. As leaders in the form of teachers, staff, and administrators, it can become very stressful to reach, teach and lead children and youth that are at-risk or have been dealt cards that they are underservant of. So, you as their parent or guardian have to tag-team with those leaders and nurture grit within them so they can grow and be passionate about life, school and everything.

You should encourage optimism.

It is okay to allow your child to fail who shows a will to win, a drive to be the best, who shows character and strength to succeed in anything he or she lay their hands on whether at home, in school, and in life. But where you will go wrong is to let him or her stay there. If they fail, it allows them to get back up and try again. I will give you an example: There was a student name Bobby (not real name) in my class who made straight A's and was the smartest one out of the rest.

He aced every test, aced every quiz I put before him, he was the first to turn in assignments and projects, he always asked me what was next after finishing his assignments in minutes. However, one day I allowed the students to test their balsa wood plane projects by flying them in an open grass area on our school campus. As we all were out in the open grassy area on a beautiful windy sunny day, all the other students were flying their planes as they all glided in the air successfully; while Bobby, on the other hand who aced everything could not.

His countenance showed immediate defeat. He began to cry every time the other students threw their planes in the air and watched them glide while his took a nose-dive. After attempting to throw his plane a few more times, he threw himself to the ground and sat there and said, "I give up." After waiting a few minutes before I went over to encourage him, he threw himself back up and tried again with another nose-dive. Then tried again with another nose-dive again. But each time, the plane went a little higher before nose-diving into the grassy ground. Each time he threw the plane, his effort and determination became stronger and stronger—making changes with how he was throwing the plane until his plane finally looked like the other students' planes—soaring into the air.

I smiled while watching him and teared up when he did not quit, although it looked like failure was all over him. This is what grit is. He failed to get his plane to soar in the air the first time, however, he did not give up, he persevered and in order to win and not fail with getting his plane to soar in the air like the other students. He was book smart but lack the smarts with social skills in how to put things together and make them work (fly).

Now he's putting robotic machines together and watching them operate. As parents, it is a must to teach our children to win in every area and if they fail, help them regroup, make changes, gather themselves when their endeavors are not working, not quit until they are completed; and they are successful with it. Bobby failed;

however, he did not stay in a failures position, he regrouped, made changes with how he was releasing the plane, gathered himself when it was not working, and did not quit until he saw the plane soaring in the air like the other students.

Sometimes we want them to excel in academics so bad that we think that's all to it in life. Well, there is way more to learn about life and how to survive in it than just making good grades. As a young girl my parents made me change a tire and I thought that was the stupidest thing they could have ever made me do. I thought that was for boys and men or for kids who like to do that. But little did I know that that was one of the best things they could have ever made me do because when I got older and owned my own car, I had a flat while driving and had to pull on the side of the road and change my tire. Although now days there is roadside assistance, my help did not come so fast. They taught me not only to study and make good grades, but they also taught me about life choices and to be independent and work hard to pursue my goals in life. I was able to change my own tire instead of waiting hours on the side of the road for someone to either come and pick me up or to change my tire. Your help may be something else, however, changing my own tire was one of mine. I am certainly not saying that my parents would come to my rescue, as they were ready to, however, they taught me, and I wanted to do it myself.

Below I have provided 8 points you can do to encourage grittiness within your children as a parent and in your students as a schoolteacher or principal:

1. Help your students, child or children find their passion. You should help them find what they love to do—what makes them happy. Not what makes you happy for them.
2. Help them to not worry about balancing their daily chores and activities. Create an organized plan for and with them (EX: Take or purchase a white erase board or poster board and make a daily plan for them to follow. Hang it up on the

wall in a place where they will go every day and use it as a guide until they begin to complete chores and activities without it).
3. You should provide constructive criticism and life lessons. Do not yell at them or control their every move and complain about the small the stuff. Do not get mad or hit them for wanting to study or go into a career that you are not in agreement with. This will only lead to withdrawal, separation or resentment.
4. Be a role model of grittiness. Don't just talk it but do it. Help provide your child or student with the strength of mind that enables them to endure pain or hardship that may rise in their lives. They are looking and need your leadership as they mature and become successful leaders themselves.
5. Praise their efforts rather than their abilities.
6. Offer challenges they can learn from.
7. Teach your children or students to handle and learn from failure.
8. Encourage them with optimism.

As a leader, teacher, coach and mentor I have noticed expecting students to be perfect is very misleading and absurd. Students learn at different compacities. They certainly do not learn when being yelled at, belittled, and ignored. Most times as I mentor, I have learned that students learn and work best when challenged with something that they are familiar with and when your approach is receivable. They do not receive and want to achieve when you are not motivating or when you are not interested in them becoming better, or when you try to act perfect as if you never make any mistakes or have or have not had any failures.

I have seen throughout my years in education many parents, teachers, staff, assistant principals, and building principals fail from the lack of compassion. When students make mistakes, they treat them as if it is the end of the world for that student. Many times, all that student needs is to know that they may make a mistake, and failure will come at one time in their lives, however, you as a parent, teacher, staff, assistant principal, and building principal must show that you care and understand, let them know that failure will come but they can learn from their failures and still become successful while still imparting discipline where needed. Also, not allow the punishment to be so harsh to where the student cannot learn from their mistakes and get better.

What Does Grit Stand for in Our Schools?

Students who are successful with grit tend to set long-term goals and never turn from them even when they do not see positive results right away. While others who are not successful tend to give up right away. People who see each other every day tend to have many different plans, witty ideas and a passion for excelling in many different ventures, however, cancel them within a few days to weeks when they do not see immediate results. Students with grit tend to set long-term goals and never turn aside of them, even when they cannot see positive change right away.

Children who practice more growth mindset have more grit—passion and perseverance to succeed when the going gets tough than those who do not.

Grit stands for building and developing culture and emphasizing character (Dean, 2014). As implementing character education within school culture is needed, throwing anything together within a character education is not likely to be successful. Grit within a curriculum should be well thought of and planned out accordingly. It should be implemented in such a way that teachers and students win in every area of its definition—the passion and perseverance to succeed no matter the cost.

Stephanie Franklin

Grit is important in our schools because it allows our students to excel and have something to work toward in their everyday lives—at home while doing chores and working on a major project they may not understand right way, or at school working on projects they like but do not understand. Students set the standard when goals they have set are met. I always believe that youth begat young. Students begat students. What this means is that students reach students as they know what it takes to be successful because they know what each other want. Children who practice more growth mindset have more grit—passion and perseverance to succeed when the going gets tough than those who do not. I love pairing my students up as they begat more students to pair up with in order to successfully complete an assignment or project. They love to compete in a positive way. It makes them stronger in faith and builds character.

In sports, students who are real gritty in sports or extra curricula activities, have each other's back. The leaders have to be mentally tough and when they are losing in a game, the leaders have to step up and be mentally tougher than their teammates, or leaders in the classroom have to be stronger than their peers. It is much different than having hectic schedules to fulfill that prevents them from moving and working toward short-term and long-term goals and visions they strive to fulfill.

What Does Grit Stand for in Your Community?

In looking at today's society of being so cold toward each other, I have found that is not always true. There are some angels that are willing and ready to help when needed. I saw more of this when the Corona COVID-19 Virus hit the globe, especially in America. The Americans pulled together to do whatever they could to help each other in need. I call this a national community.

> *The Americans pulled together to do whatever they could to help each other in need. I call this a national community.*

It was not only national; it was citywide all the way down to small communitywide. There were helpers everywhere. Mostly, I found families pulling together, coming together no matter what was between them before the epidemic. So, the question would be asked, how does this apply to grit? I will answer, being that grit is passion and perseverance, it would be a perfect fit for this time of crises and pandemic in our world.

Each school day before I began teaching my class, I always ask my students how their day is going, as they would reply "it's good," or some would begin to talk about what was bothering them, as everybody would pull together and talk about the issue seemingly finding a solution to their hurt or disagreement about something. After which, I would give my students a little pep talk because that is who I am, a motivator, inspirator, and innovator. I teach my students to be the same. But little did I know on that particular day before we left for spring break over two years ago, it would be the last time I would see them and a whole nation changed.

Corona COVID-19 came to change the world—the economy, every business and every school district there is in America and in the world. The world shifted negatively. Everything basically went virtual. If you didn't have some sort of electronic device, social network or a way to get on the internet, you were doomed. School districts scrambled to put something in place to transition to this immediate change for the betterment of our students, teachers, administrators, staff, and schools. They did a great job in doing so. I'm most proud of how my school district handled the virus and the school in which I teach. Everyone had to pull together. Everyone became a community. Everyone became a closer community. Everyone became a city-wide community. Everyone became a closer neighborhood.

So how does this apply to grit? Everyone shows grit by showing passion toward each other in need (individual and family), and everyone has and is still persevering through all of the tough times of loss of lives from the virus, loss of jobs and the frustration with having to had remained in our homes for days and months at a time. Dealing with the shortage supply of food and goods. Having to share what we have in order to help someone else. That was grit. This is what grit stands for in your community. Doing whatever it takes to help someone who is in need and persevering with them until the need is met.

Now that our schools have incorporated online learning, it is a part of your community. Families have pulled together to help each other with their children and how to teach their children the assignments given by their schools and school districts—making the best of what they have in order for their child to be successful. This is grit.

There are many different true stories of how grit is exemplified in your community. Hopefully, this will transfer on you to get busy making a difference and showing how much your community mean to you by helping someone where you live.

Below, talk about your own true stories based on the scenarios I have provided for you.

Story 1:

Talk about the teachers who have made an impact on their students virtually or in person and share with your staff and/or co-workers. If you did not do this, share what you would do in this case.

___
___
___
___
___
___
___

Story 2:

Talk about a teacher and her husband who went door to door asking each neighbor to write down what they stood in need of. For example: food or school supplies for their kids. This turned into a community-wide parade and effort to help a neighbor in need. Share this with your staff and/or co-workers. If you did not do this, share what you would do in this case.

___
___
___
___

Story 3:

Talk about how you gave toiletries, paper towels and groceries to people that needed them. How they gave to the elderly. Share this with your staff and/or co-workers. If you did not do this, share what you would do in this case.

Story 4:

Talk about how the Food Bank has been so inspirational to your community. Share this with your staff and/or co-workers. If they did not do this, share what you would do in this case.

Story 5:

Talk about how you adapted to the change from only being face-to-face to having to change your curriculum to meet expectations of virtual and face-to-face. If you did not do this, share what you would do in this case.

_____
_____
_____
_____
_____
_____
_____

TELL YOUR STORY. Everybody has a story to tell. Write below the story or stories of how you have shown grit in your school, home, community or city? Also share your pandemic time(s) during the Corona COVID-19 Virus Stay-at-Home orders within your city and community.

1.

2.

3.

4.

5.

6.

7.

8.

How Do I Make a Difference in My Community Using Grit?

One of the best ways to make a difference in your community is to believe in the community. People want someone who has a passion for people and a safe clean community environment. I always tell my students and mentees that they are not too young to give back to their community and serve their community. If we do not give back, the community will go down and there will be lack.

> **One of the best ways to make a difference in your community is to believe in the community.**

You are the community. Everyone around you is the community. It is a unified effort on everyone's part to help the community strive. You may say, I'm paying Homeowners Insurance, or property taxes, or high Homeowners Association fees, let them deal with it. Well, I understand how you feel. However, if you do not help your community, it will not flourish.

As we know grit is having the perseverance and passion to meet long-term goals and the courage to see them through, your commitment in your community means the same. You may live in an area where it seems impossible to clean it up or make it look better or get with neighbors to come up with a resolution to bring the community together. It takes planning and coming together to think of ways to either perfect or to completely clean up your neighborhood. There are many stories behind people in their communities who came together in trying circumstances, although I encourage you not to wait and if those times come, you all are encouraged to pull together.

Below is a check list to help you get started taking charge of your community and showing grit while doing it:

1. **Make a list.** Write down everything that is negative or wrong with your community.
2. **Make a plan.** Set things in order by dividing out how you are going to complete this or these goal(s). Remember to use grit as you plan because you will need perseverance if it does not work right away. Here are some examples:
    A. Clean up a vacant house, parking area or community park.
    B. Organize a can good drive for a needy family in the community.
    C. Set up a buddy system for families with special needs.
    D. Organize a food bank drive for the community for needy families.
    E. Organize tutoring for children and youth who are at home learners or those who are having trouble academically in school.
    F. Deliver meals to homebound elderly or those who are in need.
    G. Organize a group to paint over graffiti or vulgar type paintings on vacant homes or any buildings in your neighborhood or community.

H. Contact your HOA (Homeowners Association) for any ideas or questions you may have moving forward.

3. **Market your plan.** Contact your neighbors by going door-to-door letting them know what you are trying to do. You may even put-up signs with your information on it. For example, put up in the mailbox area a "Community Clean Up" sign, letting the community know that you would like to clean up the community and that it is a neighborhood community effort. You can also pass out flyers by going door-to-door providing the community and neighbors with them.
4. **Set out to accomplish your plan through grit.** Create a buddy system if needed and get everybody involved to accomplish the plan through passion for your community and perseverance to see it successfully completed even through all obstacles.

Now that you have completed your plan for your community, below I have added a clear plan for creating your foundation for action:

1. Joint down your short-term or long-term goal(s).
2. Divide your short-term or long-term goal(s) into small pieces—pieces that are easy to complete right away.
3. Review your plan everyday.
4. Stay on target with completing your short-term or long-term goal(s).
5. Contact your HOA (Homeowners Association) for any ideas or questions you may have moving forward.

21

Should Grit Be Taught in School?

It is without question that grit should be taught in schools. There are so many increments to why grit should be taught as there are so many elements that justify this statement. Students, teachers, principals, assisted principals, and staff should all play a part in this persevered attitude each school day.

We are all guilty at one point in our lives for not completing all of our individual tasks each day. While no one is perfect, there are times we may miss a to-do number on our to-do lists. I know this because I'm one of them. I have also spoken in conversation with

Exercising Grit on Your Campus Removes Cyber Bullying and Threatening Crisis.

students, teachers, and administrators that I worked with in the past and they two have mentioned that they missed completing one or two, or even more of their numbers on their to-do lists by the end of a particular day.

Exercising Grit on Your Campus Removes Cyber Bullying and Threatening Crisis

I was taking a Cybersecurity Assessment Threat Training online required by my school district while writing this book, and thought,

Stephanie Franklin

I wonder how grit applies to this subject? There must be a solution to this worldwide behavior.

As I begin to do my research and found that it does have a great deal to do with grit as there is a great need for the power of passion and perseverance for all students and the way they feel about not only their education, but also how they each feel about other students, toward the teachers they do not like, their relationship with the principals that discipline them in a way they do not agree with, and the school campus they're not in agreement with as well. It takes collaboration and a combination of leadership on our school campuses and within our school districts as a whole to be successful in this important area of concern across the globe.

I find that the secret for all students to achieve is through love, passion, and perseverance—being able to persevere with the students who show negative behavior. Each teacher, staff, and principal must watch for warning signs that a student may show if he or she is struggling in these areas. Below are a few warning signs that you can watch for:

1. A student dressing in dirty clothes that are odd. That stand out negatively.

2. Appear to be grumpy and unreachable.

3. Who does not get along with other students 99 percent of the time.

4. Who have many difficulties in school.

5. Who do not get along with his or her friends.

With my experience with working with Tier 1-3 students, Tier 3- those with at-risk behavior, these types of students may not change overnight. There is a process to change, and it takes every bit of grit to change them. If you want to see change in your at-risk students whether in your classroom or in your school, students who appear to have withdrawn behavior or students who may show anger toward your school and other students, you must be willing to love, show compassion toward how they feel even when you do not agree, and persevere with them with counseling, mentorship, social and emotional interventions and putting professional developments in place until they change. When these areas are not exercised, it can possibly open the door to the behavior of cyber bullying and threatening crises. It should be your goal as a staff and school to help all students in any way possible, and to meet their needs socially, emotionally, and academically.

I thought about why students have evil, negative feelings and hatred toward their school? Then I wondered why there are not additional professional trainings being performed at schools so that this type of behavior cannot manifest or exist. I became very sad and grieved. I have a heart and a passion for all students; especially those students who are not treated right. I began to think about my mentees. What they think and how they feel. Although I use interventions, it seems as if it's not enough for a complete school-wide change. The saying is so true, "It takes a village to raise a child." When students walk through the doors of the school, they become our responsibility. They become one of ours. The question is, what will you do with yours for the time you have each of them? Will you choose to make a difference, or will you choose to be a statistic and let them fall by the wayside? Think of them as if they were your own child or children? Would your response be different? I will leave you with that question to ponder.

Based on the training and research results, I found that it is important to always be aware when dealing with all students. You never know when a crisis or a cyber threat may occur. As it is important to interact and build a relationship with students, it is also important to observe irrational behavior that may come to harm, hurt, and bring threat to your school campus. By teaching in a gritty way, your students will learn to persevere through challenges that may occur and show passion, compassion, understanding and respect toward other students who are culturally different.

Each student is culturally different as they each have different backgrounds and home environments. Attacks can come in an instance, and it is always important to be prepared so that it will not happen on your campus.

On the next page I have created a chart that show you how to handle an escalated stage for all behaviors in different crisis.

> **How to Handle an Escalation Stage for All Behavior in Different Crisis:** *(look below)*
>
> *Calm-* The student is cooperative. The teacher and/or administrator is calm. The teacher and/or administrator should maintain a consistent peaceful environment, as they keep students calm and they will remain calm as the teacher teaches the class; and the administrator leads their daily duties throughout the school. This can also work the other way around. If the student is out of control, the teacher and/or administrator should maintain calmness with the student who is out of control until the student calms down. The teacher nor the administrator should never become hysterical and out of control with the student as this could escalate into something bigger than what they can handle. I have had to use this method when several of my students and mentees have become hysterical for various reasons with others and the calm method was used and worked successfully.

Trigger- The student is experiencing unresolved conflicts with the teacher and the teacher is experiencing unresolved conflicts with the student. A student, teacher and parent conference is appropriate to get on top of this.

Acceleration- The student and teacher maintain focused behavior. This is the time for the teacher to show and give incentives for good behavior. Let your students know that you are pleased with their behavior and class interaction.

De-Acceleration- Allow the student time to calm down time. Look for normal breathing and not hysterical breathing that is out of control.

Recovery- You would want to use positive reinforcement.

Escalating Conflicts- Escape negative conflict. Promote cooperative compliance.

Peak- Interventions that focuses and shows safety. In this situation a student has reached their peak, you should call for help and quickly remove the student. Staying as calm as possible until help comes.

Agitation- The student or teacher is experiencing unfocused behavior. It is important for the teacher to exhibit praise and positive examples to keep the students calm. Ex: *"Remember students, we are getting ready to go to*

Stephanie Franklin

> *PE, so your good behavior is important."* This statement calms the student(s) and allows them to have something positive to look forward to.
>
> Or for high school, an EX: *"Students remember I am giving extra credit points toward your lowest major grade, so your good behavior depends on it."* This statement calms the student(s) and allows them to have something positive to look forward to.

The Chart Below Shows Why Grit is Important and Should Be Taught in the Schools.

WHY NEEDED	WHAT STUDENTS LEARN
Financial Education	Teen Banking Needs
STEM, STEAM & Career Exploration	Future Goals *(short & long term)*
Social Emotional Learning	Mental, Emotional & Negative Behavior Awareness
Health & Awareness	Mental & Emotional Awareness

The Power of Grit in the Classroom, School, and Community

I have provided below a scenario that pertains to this chapter that may help you as a teacher in your classroom and/or administrator on your school campus, as you may have or will encounter this situation and need a positive breakthrough on how to handle it effectively for the success of all students and your campus.

Scenario 1:

Michael raised his hand in front of his middle school reading class while Mrs. Williams explained the assignment. She pointed at Michael as he raised his hand. "Mrs. Williams, can I be excused from this assignment?"

"I prefer you to complete this assignment Michael seeing that I am grading it." She calmly answered.

"Well, I don't understand, so I won't be completing it!" Michael blurted out with a more forced attitude.

Mrs. Williams yelled back at Michael, "calm down, it is more than you in this classroom and you've already showed out on last week with your negative behavior by yelling at me and the class because you did not understand your assignment! I will not look over your nasty attitude today!"

He yelled back, "Miss, my attitude is nasty because you won't help me but get attitudes all the time!" He got out of his seat and began to walk toward the door as if to leave.

"Where are you going?! I did not give you permission to get up out of your seat!" She yelled and rushed toward him as he started running out of the classroom yelling down the hallway, punched and broke a side window, busted through a set of double doors, and slid down the side of the brick building wall.

Ms. Williams ran back in the classroom and called for Mr. Baker, one of the assistant principals to help. When Mr. Baker came, Mrs. Williams explained her side as Mr. Baker quickly went and checked on Michael only to find him and his hand covered in blood as he was still sitting against the brick wall. Mr. Baker bent down and asked him, "What's going on buddy?"

Michael never looked up. "Mrs. Williams always gotta' get an attitude when I don't understand." He stayed looking downward towards the pavement.

Mr. Baker sat down beside Michael. "Well, it seems like something more is going on with you and Mrs. Williams and you broke school property—the window is busted."

"I didn't mean to bust out the window. She made me mad. But I am a little bit more madder cause' I was making good grades and then I couldn't understand her new assignments anymore, so I gave up."

Mrs. Williams and Mr. Baker had a meeting the next morning before school and joined Michael and his parents in on it. Michael spoke up first, "I'm sorry I yelled out at you and the class. And I'm sorry I broke the window and I understand if you want to punish me. I was always able to make straight A's in Mrs. Williams class and now I don't understand."

Mrs. Williams spoke up next, "Michael I understand your anger, and it must be frustrating when you had clear understanding and was excelling so well. It can be hard when all of that changes and seems to be taken away from you. But you must understand that I have class rules and you must follow them."

Mr. Baker cut Mrs. Williams off, "Michael there are consequences for bad behavior and for the broken window, but let's talk about how we can fix your behavior with Mrs. Williams and in her class. I hear that you were doing great at first with all A's on every one of her assignments? That is great. So, what allowed you to go down?"

"I guess I lost it when I didn't understand the work she was giving me. It's like I lost my persistence and motivation to keep it up." He paused. "But I don't wanna' quit, I wanna' start getting back where I was and making those A's again. Will you help me Mrs. Williams?" He turned and looked at her.

She smiled and calmly answered, "Michael, I sure will.... It is my job to help you to succeed and not fail. When you fail, you do not stay there, you get back up and try again. That is grit and perseverance; and you have that so use it. I apologize for raising my voice at you. My words could have been better and calmer. Neither one of us are perfect so that leaves room for us both to work together. Can we do that?"

"Yes mam', we can do that."

The meeting ended successfully with Michael and Mrs. Williams working the situation out. Mr. Baker was pleased with the meeting and how well it ended... Two weeks later, Michael began making A's again as he missed no days going to tutoring and spending one-on-one time with Mrs. Williams after school.

This scenario shows why grit is important and should be taught in schools. Many students start out strong in the beginning of the year and as the year progresses, they go down and lose their passion, perseverance and resilience to continue strong. We must understand that there is always a "why" in students and teacher's behavior. It is okay to not understand every assignment given to them, and we as parents, teachers, staff and administrators can teach students that. It is also okay to let students know that they will fall and make mistakes, but we should encourage them to build on those mistakes and not quit—that is grit. Michael started strong and lost his ability to maintain, made some bad choices, but did not quit. He bounced back and learned resilience and met his goal of making straight A's again in Mrs. Williams class. We should teach our students to be just like Michael but without his negatives. Students may make mistakes, however, with the teaching of grit and resilience, they can be encouraged to bounce back and meet short term and long goals in each one of their classes and within sports team if they are athletes as well.

Stephanie Franklin

Questions to Share with Your Class, Teen Group, and/or School:

The question is, was Michael wrong for going off on Mrs. Williams? Was he wrong for getting up out of his seat and walking out without permission? Should he have consulted with Mrs. Williams how he felt before lashing out? Was he wrong for breaking the window? Should Mr. Baker have gone outside where Michael was instead of going to Mrs. Williams class first? Should Mrs. Williams have gone outside to check on Michael? Should Mrs. Williams have gotten mad by yelling at Michael or should she have kept her composure and spoke calmly to Michael to keep him calm? Should Mrs. Williams have used the "Calm" method of behavior from the Escalation Stage for All Behavior in Different Crisis chart for this situation? Should they have had a student, parent and teacher conference? Was this scenario that serious? Were they two eventually in agreement? If this were you in this situation, what would you have done? How would you feel or react? What would you have done differently? Write your answers below and if you are in a group, mentorship session, counseling session, classroom or sports team talk about it with them.

Stephanie Franklin

The Power of Grit in the Classroom, School, and Community

Stephanie Franklin

The Power of Grit in the Classroom, School, and Community

Stephanie Franklin

Is Grit a Character Trait?

Grit is a personality trait within individuals who express passion and perseverance towards a long-term goal. This non-cognitive trait is characterized by an instinctive need to achieve objectives despite the hurdles that may come along the way.

As students work on different tasks within the classroom lesson the teacher has assigned, they may not be able to figure out what to do or understand the assignment and give up. It is important as the parent, teacher, or administrator to help the student(s) understand that it is okay to not understand the lesson and/or feel confused when learning a new lesson or project. Actually, it is beyond

Grit is a personality trait within individuals who demonstrate passion and perseverance towards a long-term goal.

normal, it is expected. Most students, or should I say, student who do not understand a new lesson right away either give up with their actions or they each give up with their eyes. I will take my students for example, there have been times when I have begun a new lesson and the students did not understand, I could literally hear a pen drop. The atmosphere shifted from conversing with one another other with excitement to learn, to long faces and total silence. Their facial expressions even changed as if they lost their favorite dog, and they moped and moaned as to say, "I don't understand." You as the teacher do not get mad at your students or become frustrated when they all gripe and complain. However, take the initiative to take it slow, and help them to take the assignment slow until they each understand. I have worked the buddy system before and turned it into a team building initiative in order to help my students and not make them feel as if they have failed and/or are failures. Reteaching may be appropriate for the success of your students.

As grit is the driver of achievement and success, without perseverance, a student, teacher, administrator, school campus, individual, parent, family, friends, business, business owner, community or world will exemplify unmet potential. Someone who is naturally talented with smarts may be great, however, to truly thrive and do well you will need perseverance. You must be determined to finish what you start even when it becomes boring after you started; or it seems harder to complete before you began. This is important to remember in terms of starting strong and finishing stronger. Not quitting when you are faced with unforeseen circumstances that may come up in your personal life or career goals.

Take the Grit Test
Below is a grit test that is only made to test you to see how gritty—persevering and passionate you are towards reaching a long-term goal that you have just made. Short-term and long-term goals are what most people struggle with. There is no answer key, and you are not a failure if you fail this test. It is not to humiliate you or to bring out the worse in you. It is only to show you how you compare to other people and the true grit that is within you. You will be able to see if you are gritty—passionate and show perseverance to see your short-and long-term goals and aspirations come true.

Let's Test Ourselves: The Character Traits	Circle True	or False
1. I never give up.	True	False
2. I do not become jealous when someone passes their test.	True	False
3. I never quit when I start a new project when it becomes boring.	True	False
4. When I do not understand something, I never give up. Instead, I ask for better understanding.	True	False
5. I can take constructive criticism when I believe that I have completed a task right.	True	False

Well, how did you do? Did you score "false" on most or all of your questions? This could be a little shaky for you as your answers should be "true" on most or all of your answers in order to be considered gritty. I suggest that you go back and reevaluate your life—lifestyle, career, approach with others, how you feel about yourself, and how you work with others. You want your answers to be all "true" in order to be considered a gritty person—passionate and showing perseverance toward short-term and long-term goals and aspirations come to past.

It is important to show compassion when we feel more resilience to keep going when times get tough or when we see a student struggle to understand the expectations of the course in which you teach. You should not take the attitude of, "o well, they'll get it and if they don't, they will just fail my class." Showing compassion with your students while you are unhappy with majority of them not passing your test, or even showing that they are not excited about being in your class. Also, showing compassion when a student is failing your class, and suddenly shows a spark of determination towards exemplifying excellence and a positive attitude toward his or her grades. There are some teachers who hold grudges because the student, who, at first was not doing anything—sleeping all the time, constantly having to tell the student to put his or her cell phone away, constant talking and up out of their seat without permission, etc. However, makes a sudden change for the better. As teachers and administrators, we should not hold grudges with students like this. We should hold them accountable, however, show compassion to help them get better; especially if they show effort in trying to change.

How do we determine the 4 Domains as they apply to our character traits? To help determine a person's character trait is to deal with their personality. Each student has a different character trait. While at school, each character trait may apply to each of the 4 domains.

Domain one- Planning and preparation applies to the teacher who prepare lessons for students and students prepare their classroom lesson or homework to turn in to the teacher. Teachers demonstrate their knowledge of the lesson and the student's interaction, feedback and passing grades show that they understood the lesson.

Domain two- The classroom environment shows a gritty atmosphere. Everyone is passionately persevering through each lesson even those who may not understand the lesson, however, is giving their all until they understand. The classroom setting shows coherent instruction and instructional outcomes that show successful students winning with the lesson.

Domain three- The instruction applies to the teacher teaching the classroom instruction in a way that gets all students involved and interacting with one another and is not taught to them in a way that makes them sleep in your class or is disruptive and making you (the teacher) have to stop teaching to tend to their negative behavior. The teacher clearly communicates with his or her students in a gritty way that allows them to push through lessons they may not understand. The students are engaged and learning effectively and successfully. The use of assessment shows their level of understanding of the instructional lesson as the teacher is flexible and responsive to the student's needs.

Domain four- The professional responsibilities occur when the teacher reflects on teaching and make sure ALL students understand how to complete the lesson that has already been taught. He or she shows this by calling parents or guardians, documenting when the students have done a great job on daily lessons and test assessment show passing grades.

On the next page is a chart showing the framework you should be following as an effective teacher in your classroom. Grit is evident as all of these are successful as the teacher is passionate about how their students feel—whether they ALL understand the lesson and are not confused. Their knowledge of the lessons shows as they all are raising their hand to answer questions rather than you having to pull the answer out of them.

The Framework for Teaching

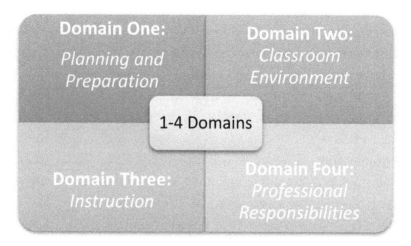

Domain One: Planning and Preparation
    a. Demonstrating knowledge of content and pedagogy
    b. Demonstrating knowledge of students
    c. Setting instructional outcomes
    d. Demonstrating knowledge of resources
    e. Designing coherent instruction
    f. Designing student assessments

Domain Two: Classroom Environment
    a. Creating an environment of respect and rapport
    b. Establishing a culture for learning
    c. Managing classroom procedures
    d. Managing student behavior
    e. Organizing physical space

Domain Three: Instruction
    a. Communicating with students
    b. Using questioning and discussion techniques
    c. Engaging students in learning
    d. Using assessment in instruction
    e. Demonstrating flexibility and responsiveness

Domain Four: Professional Responsibilities
   a. Reflecting on teaching
   b. Maintaining accurate records
   c. Communicating with families
   d. Participating in a professional community
   e. Growing and developing professionally
   f. Showing professionalism

Character traits in students reflect theses Domains. I have learned that students will let you know when they <u>do not</u> understand and when they <u>do</u> understand. Each hold their own personality and how they each come off. You as the teacher or the principal must identify this on the first day of school and learn each student for who they are. They may not come off the way you feel that they should but that does not make them wrong. By you learning them for <u>WHO</u> they are, will allow you to understand them when you present a lesson to them that they may not understand, or when they express to you that they do not understand, or sleep while you are teaching and then make adjustments for the success of your students.

It is important to build relationship with your students and learn their name and not forget it when they leave your classroom each day. I have to be honest as I am guilty of this myself at times. I am bad with learning names. I tell my students this all the time (smiling). So, instead of calling each of them by their names, I end up calling them sweetie, or young man, or young lady, or even buddy... My students love when I call them by those names, however, I am striving to get better although having almost 200 students' names to learn is not easy. Not counting the ones that are not in my class or mentor on a daily basis either.

The students on your campus are counting on you to lead and to teach them. You are their leaders and if you do not take charge and show that you care, you will never or should I say it will be very hard to get anything out of them. They will talk while you're teaching.

They will sleep while you're teaching. They will ask to go to the restroom one by one while you are teaching. They will show an increase in absents every day. They will show up to your class tardy on purpose, and disrupt it when they come in. They will smart off and make you smart off back and hope it escalates to get you in trouble. Until you lead, teach and show that you really care for them, all those things will be a negative factor. It will also leave your class destroyed by misbehavior leaving you calling for an administrator for help.

This also goes for coaches as well as those who coach sports of any kind. You must show that you care about the athletics you coach. All of them have different character traits as they all are from different cultures and backgrounds. None outshining the other. None are no better or greater than the other when it comes to caring about them. Athletes are looking for coaches who can not only coach them to be better athletes and win games, but they are also looking for a coach who really does care about them and their future. Be that coach who steps up and shines in this area with your athletes. I can remember when I was coaching freshman basketball and junior varsity at a high school I taught at years ago. I had a young lady who was one of my best players on the team. I will not share what team, however, as weeks went by and the season was just beginning, the young lady fell off by being late for practice and if she wasn't late, she did not show up at all. So, I called her and her parents and found out that she lost her self-esteem of being the best player on the team and felt that she was not good enough to lead the team. She was overwhelmed with low self-esteem and issues at home and began to feel powerless. Had I not cared enough to check on her, mentored her, encouraged her, built her back up, and let her know that her team needed her, she would have fell by the wayside and I would have never seen her again; and she would not have had a chance at a scholarship. Many times, coaches get so wrapped up in winning games that they forget about the welfare and the mentoring that boys, girls, young men, young women, and adult athletes need from you. You cannot afford to get so wrapped up in winning games alone, that you neglect your team as they need your social emotional leadership more than your expertise on how to only win games. Athletes go through tough times off the court. They are not robots—turn them on when you are ready to use them and turn them off when you are done with them until practice occurs again. You must be able to adapt to what they may be facing on a given day—academic failures, mental break downs, mom and dad splitting up, family going through a financial crisis, girlfriend or boyfriend issues, social media overload and overwhelmed responses from fans and possible stalkers, etc.

On the next pages shows Professional Developments for your staff, teachers, assistant principals, and building principals with tables of phases of school development I made up. I made them in order to encourage you to add the phases you are choosing to take your school to the next level. This area is for the teacher, assistant principal and for the building principal. You may want to meet with your skills specialist, department head and department if you are a teacher, and if you are an assistant principal and building principal, you may want to meet with your leadership team, community leaders and stakeholders before making final decisions.

Professional Developments

For Your Staff, Teachers, Assistant Principals and Building Principals

1. **PHASES OF SCHOOL DEVELOPMENT**

2. **INTERVENTIONS ON HOW TO BRIDGE THE GAP WITH RTI IN YOUR SCHOOL, AND CREATE A GRITTY ENVIRONMENT FOR LEARNING**

3. **PROFESSIONAL DEVELOPMENTS:**

    1. **Professional Development Session 1**
       District and Campus vision and T-TESS Appraisal Adventure Hunt Game

    2. **Professional Development Session 2**
       Scavenger Hunt

PROFESSIONAL DEVELOPMENT #1

PHASES OF SCHOOL DEVELOPMENT

CREATING A CULTURE FOR LEARNING:

PHASE 1 *Curriculum Content*

PHASE 2 *Methods of Student & Teacher Collaboration*

PHASE 3 *Building Improvement*

PHASE 4 *Repeat the Process*

School development should represent ongoing changes each school campus uses to promote an innovative outcome through building maintenance, teacher development—collaborative growth through curriculum and teacher morale, student development—building dialogs that encourage student morale, challenge knowledge, and promote learning.

Each phase for school development should create a culture for learning among the staff and student body. Through school development, a plan must be put in place. It needs to be a strategic plan for improvement with multiple phases. It should be clear as it brings together a simple main measure it will take to raise campus standards and increase key outcomes and targets it intends to achieve.

Every school campus should look to grow and implement phases of development that will help it to grow throughout the school year.

Too many times school campuses become too idol when things look right, and the students appear to be complying by campus rules and procedures, meaning, there are no fights, students seem to be getting to class on time without tardies, teachers are not complaining about student misbehaviors, etc.. Also, when administrators tend to pay more attention to students' negative behavior, that they neglect hidden open areas where students group up to misbehave or bring in contraband through morning metal detectors. School development is to look in areas of improvement on your school campus and among staff. It is important to have a plan in place—phases of development for your campus for student success.

I have listed 4 phases for school development.

They are:

PHASE 1: Curriculum Content.

PHASE 2: Methods of Student & Teacher Collaboration.

PHASE 3: Building Improvement.

PHASE 4: Repeat the Process. Below are overviews of each phase in more detail:

PHASE 1 OVERVIEW- *Curriculum Content*

Curriculum Content should be reviewed for improvement every chance the principal, school leadership team and each department get. 1. Start with a vision for your school and department. 2. Conduct a needs assessment. 3. Identify goals and objectives. 4. Repeat for improvement.

PHASE 2 OVERVIEW- *Methods of Student & Teacher Collaboration*

Methods of Student & Teacher Collaboration is important as students learn to collaborate and meet with other students to help create a better environment for learning on campus and student grit and morale. Teachers collaborate and meet with each other to meet consistently and consecutively to create a better environment for learning on campus, in their classrooms, within campus departments, and help build teacher grit and morale.

PHASE 3 OVERVIEW- *Building Improvement*

Building Improvement must be the main focal point of the entire campus. It is important to start with a plan and a vision to enhance and increase an environment for learning within your campus building. I have found that so many campuses are neglected in this area while others overlook this area. Instead of looking to build on an unrealistic scale, you should look to build on a small scale that your campus can handle rather than not at all. For example, build and restructure each department at a time. This could be new computer labs—order a few computers at a time, new science labs—order a few science stations at a time, new classroom equipment and furniture, paint walls, buff floors, or whatever your campus departments stand in need of.

PHASE 4 OVERVIEW- *Repeat the Process*

<u>Repeat the entire process</u> for each phase as selected students and teachers meet each week to enhance or tweak what has already been implemented. Each phase should not wait or play out until the next school year. This is an on-going phase for your campus throughout the year.

Phase 1 Overview Chart Summary in Detail

	Phase 1- Explore	Phase 2- Develop	Phase 3- Grow	Phase 4- Excel
Detailed Summary of Featured Phases *Curriculum Content*	1. Find a plan that applies with the curriculum needed on your campus. 2. Conduct and explore a needs assessment. This will be good for each department.	1. Develop a vision for the curriculum needed. 2. Identify your goal and objective for developing your departments curriculum and make it realistic to successfully complete.	1. Look for areas for improvement. Do not wait until the next school year, meet to improve throughout the year. 2. Also, repeat what you worked for and improve that.	Do not be afraid to celebrate when the vision works.

Phase 2 Overview Chart Summary in Detail

	Phase 1- Explore	Phase 2- Develop	Phase 3- Grow	Phase 4- Excel
Detailed Summary of Featured Phases *Methods of Student & Teacher Collaboration*	1. Students learn to collaborate and meet with other students to help create a better environment for learning on campus and student grit and morale. 2. Teachers collaborate and meet with each other to create	1. Develop a vision to collaborate. 2. Identify your goal and objective for developing student & teacher collaboration and make it realistic to successfully complete.	1. Look for areas for improvement. Do not wait until the next school year, meet to improve throughout the year. 2. Also, repeat what you worked for and improve that.	Do not be afraid to celebrate when the collaboration works.

	a better environment consistently and consecutively for learning on campus, in their classrooms, within campus departments and help build teacher grit and morale. 3. Conduct and explore a needs assessment.			

Phase 3 Overview Chart Summary in Detail

	Phase 1- Explore	Phase 2- Develop	Phase 3- Grow	Phase 4- Excel
Detailed Summary of Featured Phases *Building Improvement*	1. Find a plan that applies with the building improvement that must be the main focal point of the entire campus. 2. Conduct and explore a needs assessment. When is it needed? Where is it needed?	1. Develop a vision for building improvement. 2. Identify your goal and objective for developing your campus building improvement and make it realistic to successfully complete. 3. Start with the small building	1. Look for areas for improvement. Do not wait until the next school year, meet to improve throughout the year. 2. Build and restructure each department at a time. 3. Also, repeat what you worked	Do not be afraid to celebrate when the vision works.

The Power of Grit in the Classroom, School, and Community

| | *Why is it needed?* | *equipment and small maintenance areas in the building that need improvement.* | *for and improve that.* | |

Phase 4 Overview Chart Summary in Detail

	Phase 1- Explore	**Phase 2- Develop**	**Phase 3- Grow**	**Phase 4- Excel**
Detailed Summary of Featured Phases *Repeat the Process*	*1. Find a plan that applies with the building improvement that must be the main focal point of the entire campus.* *2. Conduct and explore a needs assessment.*	*1. Develop a vision for building improvement.* *2. Identify your goal and objective for developing your campus building improvement and make it realistic to successfully complete.*	*1. Look for areas for improvement. Do not wait until the next school year, meet to improve throughout the year.* *2. Build and restructure each department at a time.* *3. Also, repeat what you worked for and improve that.*	*Do not be afraid to celebrate when the vision works.*

193

NOW You Create Your Own Phase of School Development for Your Campus:

Create A Culture for Learning for your
Classroom or Campus- (For Fall & Spring)

PHASE 1 OVERVIEW

PHASE 2 OVERVIEW

PHASE 3 OVERVIEW

PHASE 4 OVERVIEW

Phase 1 Overview Chart in Detail

	Phase 1- Explore	Phase 2- Develop	Phase 3- Grow	Phase 4- Excel

Phase 2 Overview Chart in Detail

	Phase 1- Explore	Phase 2- Develop	Phase 3- Grow	Phase 4- Excel

Phase 3 Overview Chart in Detail

	Phase 1- Explore	Phase 2- Develop	Phase 3- Grow	Phase 4- Excel

Phase 4 Overview Chart in Detail

	Phase 1- Explore	Phase 2- Develop	Phase 3- Grow	Phase 4- Excel

PROFESSIONAL DEVELOPMENT #2

> ## INTERVENTIONS ON HOW TO BRIDGE THE GAP WITH RTI IN YOUR SCHOOL, AND CREATE A GRITTY ENVIRONMENT FOR LEARNING
>
> **INTERVENTION 1   INTERVENTION 2   INTERVENTION 3**

Within this Professional Development 2 you will group up with your department, or you will follow the professional development facilitator as they instruct you to take a number from a box and whatever number you choose, you will group up with the persons with the same number. You have about 30-45 minutes to complete this professional development. If need be, you may choose your time limits.

What will the teacher, principal, assistant principal, and staff learn from this professional development?

The teacher, principal, assistant principal and staff will learn how and why bridging the gap with RTI in your school and creating a gritty environment in your classroom and school is important and contributes greatly to the success of your students.

Instructions:

The teacher, principal, assistant principal, and/or staff, as they are in their chosen groups, **will create their own RTI interventions** for their **department-** (skills specialist, department chair and teachers), **school-** (teachers, administrators and campus leaders), and/or **classroom-** (for teachers, teacher aides, inclusion teachers, ELA (English Language Arts) teachers, and/or ELL (English Language Learners) teachers, Special Education teachers).

They may use their phones and/or Chrome Books to do research and the facilitator will provide a PowerPoint about RTI and how interventions are created. <u>The facilitator will create 5 clue cards with only the questions on them and set them on each table</u> the teachers, principals and staff will be sitting at. Do not add the answers on the clue cards as this will allow the teachers, principals and staff to collaborate with each other to find the answers and learn them for themselves. Only the facilitator will have a slide presentation provided or a well typed answer card provided for review after the 30–45 minute time limit is up or the given time you set is up.

QUESTIONS & ANSWERS (<u>*FOR FACILITATORS ONLY*</u>: *Do not give answers or provide the answers to those participating. Only provide them with the questions until time is up).*

Question 1:
What is RTI and what does the abbreviation stand for?

Answer 1:
Response to Intervention (RTI) is a multi-tier approach to the early identification and support of students with learning and behavior needs (Google, (2021).

****Now discuss how you and your group use it in your class and with your students.*

Question 2:
Why is learning, knowing and using RTI important?

Answer 2:
RTI is a process that is used to help students who may be struggling with negative behavior, a skill, or academics. Every teacher will use interventions (a set of teaching procedures particularly represented within their lesson plans), with their student(s) to help meet the need and to help them to be successful in their classroom. This is not just for the student who have a special need or a disability, it is for all students no matter the color, race, or gender.

***Now discuss how you and your group use it in your class and with your students.*

Question 3:
What are the 3 Tiers of RTI?

Answer 3:
1. *Tier 1- The whole class.*
2. *Tier 2- Small group interventions.*
3. *Tier 3- Intensive interventions.*

***Now discuss how you and your group use it in your class and with your students.*

Question 4:
What are RTI Interventions?

Answer 4:

RTI Interventions are building relationships, adapting the environment, managing sensory stimulation, changing communication strategies, providing prompts and clues, using a teach, review, and reteach process, and developing social skills.

Example: A student who is having trouble understanding sentence structure and needs additional support. The teacher gives feedback by providing a lesson they understand. The student may need help with run-on sentences. The RTI example may be for the teacher to use alternative modalities of learning.

Question 5:
What are the benefits of using RTI?

Answer 5:
- *The benefits of using RYI is that it ensures that all students receive first-class instruction in their understanding and in the classroom.*
- *It ensures that all principals, assistant principals, counselors, and teachers provide and promote immediate intervention as soon as it is identified that the student's behavior and academic difficulties are hindered from developing.*

Below are some sample interventions for various departments you can also use as interventions within your district and/or campus professional developments:

SAMPLE READING TEACHER INTERVENTION:

The reading teacher will use a great method with students as they will use the:

- **Read Out Loud and the Wordless Treatment.** What this means is the reading teacher will read out loud to their students as the students follow along using the wordless treatment, meaning no words at all. They all are totally quiet—they will not comment or ask questions pertaining to what the teacher is reading to them.
- **Echo Reading-** What this means is the students will repeat what the teacher has read for understanding and clarity.
- **Paired Reading-** What this means is the teacher will pair two students with each other and have them read to each other aloud for understanding and clarity.
- **Listening Performance-** What this means is the teacher will watch each student closely to make sure they understood.
- **Repeated Reading-** What this means is the teacher will make the students repeat what the teacher read for understanding and clarity.

Please Note: This can work the same with other core and elective courses.

SAMPLE MATH TEACHER INTERVENTION:

The math teacher will use a great method with students as they will use the:

- Use the hallway method to create math solutions with math mazes on the walls and along the floor as the student's problem solve to find the solutions to the answers.

- Use small groups (2 or 3 students) and problem solve.
- Use effective mathematical teaching practices that incorporates strategies that include systematic and specific instruction. Visual representation is important — manipulatives, pictures and graphs, and relationships and functions.
- Use the board and wall sticky method with clarity and understandable problems and instruction.
- Trio (3) grouping for small group problem solving.
- Create stations with small groups and spread stations all over the classroom as students will visit each station solving problems together and then moving on to next station until completed.
- Systematic and unequivocal instruction.
- Formative assessment that is on-going.
- Changing environment inside classroom to outside (your school track, open field, sidewalk, school cafeteria, school gym, etc.) game related problem-solving interventions.

PLEASE NOTE: This can work the same with other core and elective courses.

Below Are More Interventions You Can Use in Your Classroom:

1. *Students meeting in small groups in the classroom and working as a group on the same thing.*
2. *Providing student individual lessons and repeatedly asking for understanding.*
3. *Provide a separate resource classroom only used for those students who need additional help and intervention help.*

4. NG Intervention help classroom. Used to help students who battle with coming to school and completing all course work successfully. This room will be used for sessions and only for a period of time, as the successful student will graduate from this intervention and go on to regular classes once completed.
5. Identify. Screen. Monitor. The teacher will identify and screen for assessments to identify which students require additional help and support. The teacher will monitor the progress each student has made using a measure of effective instruction and progress to all goals.
6. The teacher, principal, assistant principal, counselor and staff can use _diverse learning_.
7. The teacher, principal, assistant principal, counselor and staff can use _inquiry-based learning_.
8. The teacher, principal, assistant principal, counselor and staff can use _game-based learning_ (great for student building activities).
9. The teacher, principal, assistant principal, counselor and staff can use _active Learning_.
10. The teacher, principal, assistant principal, counselor and staff can use _cooperative Learning_.
11. The teacher, principal, assistant principal, counselor and staff can use _experiential Learning_.
12. The teacher, principal, assistant principal, counselor and staff can use _problem Solving_.

Now create your own interventions for your department, classroom and/or mentor group or program.

INTERVENTION 1
Department: **Classroom:**   **Mentor Group or Mentor Program**

INTERVENTION 2

Department:

Classroom:

Mentor Group or Mentor Program

INTERVENTION 3

Department:

Classroom:

Mentor Group or Mentor Program

YOUR ADDITONAL NOTES ON INTERVENTIONS:

Department:

Classroom:

Stephanie Franklin

Mentor Group or Mentor Program:

PROFESSIONAL DEVELOPMENT #3

> **Professional Development #3,** *Session 1*
> District and Campus Vision and
> T-TESS Appraisal Adventure Hunt Game
>
> Professional Development #3, Session 2
> *Scavenger Hunt*
>
> Professional Development #3, Session 2
> *Virtual Scavenger Hunt*

Professional Development *Session 1*

Get in a group of three or four, grab some blank clue cards and a pencil, pen, or marker; and <u>add the questions below only on one side of the cards.</u> <u>On the other side you will write the answers that your group have answered as you pass the clue cards around to each other</u>. Do not add your name or the group name on the clue cards. It is not important to find out who has the right answer. No one is shining at this point. It is a group effort as everyone is winning and encouraged to interact and share. Within about 5-10 minutes, each group will all share their answers with the entire staff or faculty present. Answers should line up with your campus vision, instructional short-term and long-term goals, and T-TESS rubric and appraisal. See the next page for questions and answers.

Questions & Add Your Answers Below:

Question   Add Your Answer

1. What do you think districts should do differently to find and hire high-quality teachers and principals?

2. What would make a teacher remain or leave a job?

3. Reflecting on a recent lesson you observed or delivered that was effective, what occurred during that lesson that led it to be effective to you?

4. Name the 4 Dimensions listed in the T-TESS Rubric.

5. Write your idea of your Campus Vision?

6. What are your instructional short-term goals?

7. What are your instructional long-term goals?

8. On the T-TESS Rubric, what does the "LEARNING ENVIRONMENT DIMENSION 3.2 Managing Student Behavior" establishes?

9. What are the Appraisal Guidelines (T-TESS) and what role do they play? ⇐

10. What is your final Campus Vision that all the staff came up with? ⇐

PLEASE NOTE: ANSWERS 4, 8, AND 9 CAN BE FOUND AT THE BACK OF THE BOOK.

Add your thoughts on cue cards to these statements below. You may also write in the box below as well. (The facilitator will pass out cue cards as the teachers and staff will write their thoughts regarding the statements below as an exercise). Provide 10-15 minutes for them to complete it and discuss all answers when time is up.

PROVIDE- more teacher and staff pay

OFFER- more professional development with more teacher respect

IMPROVE- teacher and student connecting individually

PROVIDE- outreach support and training

INCREASE- high expectations of all students regardless of their previous academic performance.

Stephanie Franklin

ADDITIONAL Cue Card Statements: *(Write your thoughts from these statements on a cue card and then share with your group and staff).*

1. Inculcating a spirit of inquiry in students.
2. Enabling purposeful parental involvement in your class.
3. Accepting all students, no matter the race, creed, or academic level.

Professional Development #3, *Session 2*
Scavenger Hunt

A scavenger hunt can motivate teachers, staff and administrators to work together as a team, learn each other, build culture among them and cause them to collaborate to complete a task. Scavenger hunts can help break the ice, introduce new staff and make professional development days more engaging.

This Professional Development #3, *Session 2 (Campus)* Scavenger Hunt should be led by a facilitator (appointed school leader or administrator) who will explain the reason for the scavenger hunt, why it is needed and what the outcome goals are. She or he will also give instructions on how it should be played.

This Professional Development #3, *Session 2 (Virtual)* Scavenger Hunt is a game in which the teacher, staff and assistant principal seek to gather or complete items on an organized list on your school campus or online (virtually). They each will work within small teams within the scavenger hunt. This allows them to actively engage, collaborate with each other, build teacher and staff morale and culture within the staff; and take them out of their comfort zones of sitting all day at tables.

Leader Expectations:
There is a high expectation for the principal, assistant principals, the leadership team, skills specialist, the department chair, janitorial leader, and lead cook.

Scavenger Hunt Question:
Who Knows Your Campus Vision and Your Department Vision the Best?

Stephanie Franklin

Scavenger Hunt Theme:
District vision, campus vision, campus department vision, and T-TESS (Texas Teacher Evaluation and Support System) is important for teachers and staff to know.

Scavenger Hunt Place:
School library, gym or cafeteria.

Scavenger Hunt Goal:
The goal of this Scavenger Hunt is to know and understand what your campus vision and department vision stands for, build teamwork, see visual collaboration among the staff and help you better follow the campus vision and the vision for your department throughout the school year successfully.

Scavenger Hunt Instructions (for Library, gym or cafeteria):
For the Scavenger Hunt Professional Development #3- *Session 2* Game, you will begin in your school library, gym or cafeteria. After the instructions, your entire campus staff/faculty or department will go throughout the entire campus finding the answers to the clues provided. I recommend that you do this part of your professional development last considering it will take the longest to complete. The first team who completes every Scavenger Hunt Level, answers, and puts all the clues together, wins. Your team must stay together, no one (individual) can wonder off or go ahead and find the answers on their own. In order to move to the next room or place (level), the team must successfully conquer that level they are on and take the "*Scavenger Hunt Level Completed Successfully Coin.*"

After conquering a level, collect all coins, complete each level within the entire Scavenger Hunt and return back to the library, gym or cafeteria starting point. If the team is not successful at a certain or all Scavenger Hunt Level(s), they will receive a "*Scavenger Hunt Level*

The Power of Grit in the Classroom, School, and Community

<u>NOT Completed Successfully Coin</u>." Receiving this paper coin will count against their chances of winning the Scavenger Hunt.

It is a team effort and will cause each team to collaborate by working together. I have learned that when the department lines up and are aligned with the campus vision, the school flourishes, the needs of students are met, and students, staff, teachers, assistant principals, and head principals are successful every day.

Let's see the Scavenger Hunt in step-by-step format for the facilitator leading the Scavenger Hunt:

1. <u>Number each table</u> before faculty and staff come in your library, gym or cafeteria.
2. <u>Prepare and have a list of teachers and staff names</u> with the team number they will be located on the outside of the library, gym or cafeteria.
3. <u>You will put the faculty and staff in teams of 4, 5 or 8,</u> (the number may increase or decrease depending on the faculty and staff size):

   Team 1 will begin at table 1,
   Team 2 will begin at table 3,
   Team 3 will begin at table 7,
   Team 4 will begin at table 6,
   Team 5 will begin at table 4,
   Team 6 will begin at table 10,
   Team 7 will begin at table 8,
   Team 8 will begin at table 2,
   Team 9 will begin at table 5, and
   Team 10 will begin at table 9.

4. You will select a <u>team leader</u>, a <u>team secretary-</u> who will keep the notes, and a <u>team timer-</u> who will keep time.
5. <u>You will have only 15 minutes at each designated place (level)</u> to completely answer the clues successfully. If you conquer the

level correctly you will receive a *"Scavenger Hunt Level Completed Successfully Coin"* and go on to the next Scavenger Hunt level. If you do NOT conquer that level, your team will have to remain at that Scavenger Hunt station/table/level until you all answer the clue correctly. If your team never answers the clue correctly, you all will move to the next Scavenger Hunt level without credit for completing that level correctly within the amount of time limit given (15 minutes) and will have to get the *"Scavenger Hunt Level NOT Completed Successfully Coin"* before leaving that level. The team timer will tell the team secretary the time you all completed that level and take the *"Scavenger Hunt Level NOT Completed Successfully Coin."*

6. You will go from Scavenger Hunt level to level and read the clue cards that will be placed in a secret designated place the facilitator has placed them (you as the facilitator will explain where or how to find the clue cards and clues in each station/table/level).

7. Once you find the clue card, you will read it and do exactly what it tells you to do until you have conquered what is on the clue card for that designated level.

8. The set up should allow room for each team to read the clue card if they show up at that station/table/level at the same time, or if a team gets stuck and needs more time to answer the clue correctly. Make sure the clue cards and the activity for that designated area are not located under each other to avoid over crowdedness.

9. Other teams can pass the team that is stuck on a clue if they are too slow. May the best team or department win.

The Clue Cards is located on the next page.

Table 1- Clue Card 1
(Write the question below on a clue card and set it on a table).

Question:

Student Social Behavior- What is social behavior of students?
Hint- Google may be able to help you.

Answer:

(Answer is only shown to your <u>facilitator and/or administrator</u> who is leading the scavenger hunt). Social behavior was broadly defined as including social skills deficits, behavior under inadequate stimulus control, and inappropriate behavior in the classroom.

Table 2- Clue Card 2
(Write the question below on a clue card and set it on a table).

Question:

Time Management- Know when it's time to quit. What time does dismissal begins each school day? What are your teacher and student procedures?

Answer:

Dismissal begins at (your school time) each school day unless inclement weather permits.

The principal's secretary (or chosen staff) will release each class by hallway over the PA System. Teacher and student procedure is to stop their class lessons and prepare to leave, follow the secretary (or chosen staff) instructions and when their hallway is called they will all leave going to the bus ramp. The students will get on their buses or leave as a car rider, teachers will stay on bus ramp for bus duty until told to leave.

Table 3- Clue Card 3-
(Write the question below on a clue card and set it on a table).

Question:

TechnoSTEAM Career & Technology- How well do you know STEAM *(Science, Technology, Engineering, Art, and Math)* and your technology labs?

Answer:

You will relocate to a technology lab on your campus and without touching anything, you will take an individual photo of a computer mouse, keyboard, monitor and the entire team with the technology lab in the background. You will take a creative team photo demonstrating and exemplifying something about how technology works and is important. Your team will put these items in a slide show, and upload the slide show to your Google drive, and prepare to show the faculty and staff when you all rejoin back together in the library, gym, or cafeteria or after the scavenger hunt is completed.

Table 4- Clue Card 4
(Write the question below on a clue card and set it on a table). You will need to put several copies of your district's Student/Parent Handbook on this table.

Question:
Dress Code- What student dress items are appropriate and inappropriate for school? What are the first five proper attire for all students? *Hint: Student/Parent Handbook.*

Answer:
The facilitator or administrator will add their Student/Parent Handbook answer. Answer is encouraged to fall under your topic of "Proper Attire for all Students" in the Student/Parent Handbook.

Table 5- Clue Card 5
(Write the question below on a clue card and set it on a table).

Question:
T-TESS -vs- Invest- How is T-TESS different from Invest? *Hint: T-TESS and Invest should be your ultimate search.*

Answer:
You will find the answer on your district website.

Table 6- Clue Card 6
(Write the question below on a clue card and set it on a table).

Question:

Importance of T-TESS- Why did the district shift from Invest to T-TESS?

Answer:

You will find the answer on your district website.

Table 7- Clue Card 7
(Write the question below on a clue card and set it on a table).

Question:

Students Favorite Gathering Spot- Where on your campus does the students like to gather up together for breakfast and lunch?

Answer:

Take a photo of your teammates in the spot where the students gather for breakfast and lunch. Upload the photo to your Google Drive to show when everyone reassembles.

Table 8- Clue Card 8
(Write the question below on a clue card and set it on a table).

Question:

Morning Duty- Is teacher and staff morning duty important? Why?

Answer:

Yes, teacher morning duty is important because teacher, staff and administrators should monitor and facilitate behavior and help students follow campus rules and guidelines.

To show that you know your answer is right, your team will take a photo in your cafeteria in front of a metal detector on your campus. The photo must show all of you actively monitoring during morning duty within your morning duty spots and metal detectors. Upload the photo to your Google Drive to show when everyone reassembles.

Table 9- Clue Card 9
(Write the question below on a clue card and set it on a table).

Question:

1. **Safety-** Are you required to wear a mask at school?
2. What is **Shelter-In-Place**?

Answer:

In the case of a Hazmat situation, students and staff would be directed to close their windows, shut down their heating and air conditioning units, and seal windows and doors to preserve the good inside air while restricting the entry of any contaminated outside air.

Stephanie Franklin

Table 10- Clue Card 10
(Write the question below on a clue card and set it on a table).

Take a photo showing that your group/team is all in and are excited about starting the school year off successful!

Upload all photos to your Google Drive and be ready to present them to the rest of the staff and faculty when you all reunite back together to complete your professional development.

NOTE: You may add more tables and more clue cards if you have a larger size faculty and/or employee staff.

Professional Development #3, *Session 2*
Scavenger Hunt

VIRTUAL

If you are teaching your students or child remotely (virtually) and are looking for ways to get them engaged, a Google Meet or Zoom scavenger hunt is a great idea for students, parents, or anyone that want to have fun. A Google Meet or Zoom scavenger hunt can be used to reinforce educational standards and for educational purposes. Scavenger hunt online games can also be used to teach social-emotional learning (SEL) students, or as a fun way to get your students or children to interact while social distancing.

The VIRTUAL Professional Development #3, *Session 2* Scavenger Hunt requires the participating individuals and/or teams to utilize their home, garage, or office to complete each scavenger hunt level below.

Each student or individual will search for items in their home, garage, or office and then share what they find virtually. Below are the steps for the virtual scavenger hunt:

1. Tell what to find or give a clue.
2. Set a timer to 30 to 60 seconds.
3. Students, individuals and/or parents will go and look for an item to go with the clue.

Students or individuals must be sitting in their seats with their items when the timer goes off or they are disqualified from the round. This prevents the game from lasting forever and having the rest of the class waiting for one student.

Stephanie Franklin

Students or individuals share their findings.

Another option is to give students or individuals a list of items and set the timer for a longer period of time. Then, students, individuals or team search as many items from the list as possible within the given amount of time.

SCAVENGER HUNT LEVEL 1- QUE CARD 1

Find an educational book in your home and find an educational sentence in the book and read it to your teacher or parent. If more than one individual, team or each team finds an educational book at the same time or within the allotted time, they will choose the best one out of them all.

SCAVENGER HUNT LEVEL 2- QUE CARD 2

Find a car or truck tire jack. If more than one individual, team or each team finds a car or truck tire jack at the same time or within the allotted time, they will choose the best one out of them all.

SCAVENGER HUNT LEVEL 3- QUE CARD 3

Find 5 small paper clips. If more than one team or each team finds 5 small paper clips at the same time or within the allotted time, they will choose the first one out of the team who finds it first.

SCAVENGER HUNT LEVEL 4- QUE CARD 4

Find a bottle of shampoo and a bottle of conditioner. If more than one team or each team finds a bottle of shampoo, a bottle of conditioner at the same time or within the allotted time, they will choose the first one out of the team who finds it first.

Gritty Goals

For the Teacher

GRITTY GOALS FOR THE TEACHER
SHORT TERM GOALS ONLY

Add short term goals for your students

Add short term goals for your classroom (virtual or face-to-face on your campus)

Add short term goals for you as a teacher

Add short term goals for your department

GRITTY GOALS FOR THE TEACHER
LONG TERM GOALS ONLY

Add long term goals for your students

Add long term goals for your classroom (virtual or face-to-face on your campus)

Add long term goals for you as a teacher

Add long term goals for your department

Gritty Goals

For the Principal

GRITTY GOALS FOR THE PRINCIPAL
SHORT TERM GOALS ONLY

Add short Term Goals for your students

Add short term goals for your classroom (virtual or face-to-face on your campus)

Add short term goals for you as a teacher

Add short term goals for department

GRITTY GOALS FOR THE PRINCIPAL
LONG TERM GOALS ONLY

Add long term goals for your students

Add long term goals for your classroom (virtual or face-to-face on your campus)

Add long term goals for you as a teacher

Add long term goals for department

Stephanie Franklin

Why is Corporative Learning Important to Setting Gritty Goals?

COOPERATIVE LEARNING

Why is cooperative learning important for teachers & your students? How does it apply to grit?

Cooperative learning helps the teacher to accomplish short term and long-term goals in their classroom. It is used in a collaborative way as it allows students to construct knowledge, provide an opportunity for them to practice and develop communication skills, and prepares them for real life and the real working world. It applies to grit as it allows students to dig deep in their learning compacity and come out with gritty outcomes that allow them to be successful with each assignment and their overall grade in each class.

Examples of Cooperative Learning:

1. **Turn-to-Your-Neighbor:** The teacher puts students into pairs and prompts them to turn to their partner and share with each other what they are learning. This is led by the teacher as the students are following.
2. **Think. Pair. Share:** The student writes their thoughts on a sheet of paper, shares it with another student, and then shares what they have written with the larger class for discussion.
3. **Jigsaw:** The students are divided into small groups as each group learns a fraction of the content being taught in class, then, after the teacher assigns students to other new groups, they will talk about what they have learned. *(See the Elliot Aronson's Jigsaw cooperative learning technique I have learned a lot from below).*

The Jigsaw Classroom Cooperative Learning Technique-

The Jigsaw Classroom is a cooperative learning technique thought of by Elliot Aronson, (1971) that reduces racial conflict among school children, promotes better learning, improves student motivation, and increases enjoyment of the learning experience (Jigsaw Classroom, 1971).

JIGSAW CLASSROOM IN 10 EASY STEPS

The jigsaw classroom is very simple to use. If you're a teacher, just follow these steps:

STEP ONE
Divide students into 5- or 6-person jigsaw groups. The groups should be diverse in terms of gender, ethnicity, race, and ability.

STEP TWO
Appoint one student from each group as the leader. Initially, this person should be the most mature student in the group.

STEP THREE
Divide the day's lesson into 5-6 segments. For example, if you want history students to learn about Eleanor Roosevelt, you might divide a short biography of her into stand-alone segments on: (1) Her childhood, (2) Her family life with Franklin and their children, (3) Her life after Franklin contracted polio, (4) Her work in the White House as First Lady, and (5) Her life and work after Franklin's death.

STEP FOUR
Assign each student to learn one segment. Make sure students have direct access only to their own segment.

STEP FIVE
Give students time to read over their segment at least twice and become familiar with it. There is no need for them to memorize it.

STEP SIX
Form temporary "expert groups" by having one student from each jigsaw group join other students assigned to the same segment. Give students in these expert groups time to discuss the main points of their segment and to rehearse the presentations they will make to their jigsaw group.

STEP SEVEN
Bring the students back into their jigsaw groups.

STEP EIGHT
Ask each student to present her or his segment to the group. Encourage others in the group to ask questions for clarification.

STEP NINE
Float from group to group, observing the process. If any groups are having trouble (e.g., a member is dominating or disruptive), make an appropriate intervention. Eventually, it's best for the group leader to handle this task. Leaders can be trained by whispering an

> instruction on how to intervene, until the leader gets the hang of it.
>
> **STEP TEN**
> At the end of the session, give a quiz on the material. Students quickly come to realize that these sessions are not just fun and games but really count.

4. **Value Line:** Is where the teacher presents a topic, issue, or question to their students and then assigns a value to each thinkable response. The teacher asks their students to formulate a line based on how they respond once the students line up. The teacher is in control and guides a discussion about the topic with their students.
5. **Round Table:** Is a form of a discussion in an academic way. Students agree concerning a specific topic to discuss and debate about. Each person has a right to share and is given that right by the teacher. Picturing a circular layout which is referred to the term as "round table."

    The students will get in groups. Each student will write down a question on their sheet of paper and then pass their paper to the student to the right of them and keeps going until each student have had an opportunity to answer a question. This is also a great technique for ELA (English Language Learners) classes.

    The teacher will use a timer and an overhead projector. The teacher helps to keep the discussion moving along and on task as she or he provides needed time for students to discuss the supporting questions. This will help the students debate about the topic and come to a consensus on whether

Stephanie Franklin

to do a "pro" or a "con" approach.

An example of *Round Table* is to take a topic like the question on stocks and bonds. The supporting argument would ask: "What are the arguments for stocks and bonds?" The chosen student moderator repeats the question and asks each student for their response, asks for evidence and reasoning. Each student is told to record other responses along with theirs. The next question may ask "What are the arguments against stocks and bonds?" The process is followed the same way again.

This discussion can be collaborated over a period of time, or within 3-4 classroom settings. However, the teacher chooses.

Below is a diagram of what the round table looks like:

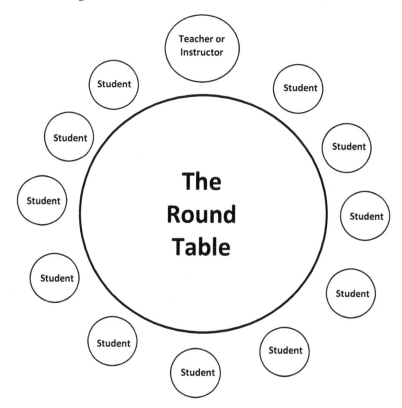

What are some examples of cooperative learning on your campus? Write them below. If they are the same, please elaborate.

Stephanie Franklin

Checklist: Cooperative Learning Success Factors

(Add a check ✓ if you agree and the statement applies to you)

Success Factors	✓
The teacher clearly understands the learning structure.	
The teacher has created a safe environment.	
The teacher has written expectations for how students should act, talk, and move while they perform the cooperative learning activity.	
Students have learned the expectations for how to act, talk, and move during the cooperative learning activity.	
Students have learned and use appropriate social skills to ensure they interact positively and effectively during the activity.	
Reading teacher has carefully considered the optimal makeup of each group of students.	
The teacher has given students sufficient time for each activity, without providing so much time that the learning loses intensity.	
Students have additional activities they can do if they finish their tasks before others.	
The teacher has planned additional activities to use during the class if activities take less time than planned.	
The teacher has planned how to adjust the lesson plan if activities take more time than planned.	
The teacher uses an effective attention signal.	

Checklist: Turn-To-Your-Neighbor

Students know…	√
Who their learning partner will be before they start.	
What tasks, if any, they need to do before they turn to their neighbor.	
What tasks they need to do with their partner (e.g., confirm their understanding, compare answers, and share an opinion).	
The outcome they need to produce for the class (e.g., a written product, a comment to share with the class, thumbs up) at the end of the conversation.	
How they should communicate with each other (in particular, how they should listen and talk).	

Checklist: Think, Pair, Share

Students know …	√
Who their learning partner will be before they start.	
Exactly what the thinking prompt is to which they are responding.	
How much time they will have to write their response.	
That they are to use all the time they are given to think and write about their response.	
The outcome they need to produce for the class (e.g., a written product, a comment to share with the class, thumbs up) at the end of the conversation.	
How they should communicate with each other (in particular, how they should listen and talk).	

Checklist: Jigsaw

Students know …	√
What group they will be in for the first activity (perhaps by writing down the number for their group).	
What group they will be in for the second activity (again, perhaps by writing down the number for their group).	
How they are to work together to learn and summarize what they are learning.	
The product they need to create to share with the second group.	
Before moving to the second group, that what they have created has received their teacher's stamp of approval.	
How they should communicate with each other in both groups (how they should listen and talk).	
How they will record (usually take notes or fill out a learning sheet) what they learn from their fellow students in their second group.	

Checklist: Value Line

Students know …	√
The question that they are considering.	
How much time they have to consider the question?	
Where the numbers for the value line are located in the room.	
Why they are being asked to line up in a value line.	
When they should move and how quickly.	

What they should talk about and how loud they should talk.	
What they should do when they get to their spot on the number Line.	

Checklist: Round Table

Students know ...	√
Each question they are responding to.	
How much time they have to consider the question?	
Where they are to pass the paper.	
How they will sum up what they have learned or discovered.	
How they will share what they have learned with the rest of the class.	

Synthesis & Take Action

For Teachers...

1. Think about your upcoming week. Where within your lesson can you incorporate a discussion among your students about the norms?
2. Ask your students to think about and reflect on a learning target: "I understand how my personal actions and choices help me be a better student, school and community leader." Now come up with a conclusion for your students to learn from.
3. Think about misbehaviors you have had in your classroom. What would you believe would be respectful, realistic, relevant, irrational, rational, well-deserved consequences for those behaviors?

Stephanie Franklin

Below is where you write your answers...

1. _____
   _____
   _____
   _____
   _____
   _____
   _____
   _____
   _____
   _____
   _____
   _____
   _____
   _____
   _____
   _____
   _____
   _____
   _____

2. _____
   _____
   _____
   _____
   _____
   _____
   _____
   _____
   _____
   _____
   _____
   _____
   _____
   _____
   _____

3. _____
   _____
   _____
   _____

_____
_____
_____
_____
_____
_____
_____
_____
_____
_____
_____

For School leaders...
1. Be the best leader on your school campus vision, code of conduct or school character traits (student characteristics, qualities, or behavior). Explain what is your next step(s) with your staff in connecting these norms (rules, standards, models, patterns) on your campus and in each classroom?
2. It is important for school faculty to embrace the same school vision and campus and classroom values to model them for students to be successful. It is required that teachers and administrators work together as a team to show and name what that vision and those campus and classroom values are and show what they look like. Create a professional development or a faculty and staff meeting agenda that will focus on faculty values and norms (rules, standards, models, patterns) and show how your teachers and administrators will incorporate it within their classrooms and school campus.
3. As a leader on your school's leadership committee, you hear about a first-year biology teacher who is struggling in the classroom. The teacher was put on a growth plan. You were just asked to mentor this teacher. What steps will you take in helping this teacher to be successful in the classroom? And to avoid potential release at the end of the school year?
4. You as an assistant principal conducts a teacher's appraisal and rates the teacher's appraisal with a score that does not meet expectations. The teacher is furious and emails the building

principal right away. How should you come to resolve this problem? If you are a building principal, how would you resolve this problem?

Below is where you write your answers...

1. _____

2. _____

3.

4.

Additional Writing Space below:

THE SPACE BELOW IS USED FOR YOUR PROFESSIONAL DEVELOPMENT OR FACULTY MEETING AGENDA

The Power of Grit in the Classroom, School, and Community

The Power of Grit in the Classroom, School, and Community

The Power of Grit in the Classroom, School, and Community

Self-Awareness Activities

These are self-awareness activities that you can do with all your students, mentees or athletes. I have done these with my mentees in my mentor program, my classroom students, and my athletes when I was coaching; and they were very effective. In fact, the students, mentees and athletes turned from their negative behavior to positive behavior in a short period of time. It made my classroom and team closer and helped with setting a positive environment for learning and accomplishing their goals. I have learned that when you feel good about yourself, others will know it and it will transfer on them to feel the same way about themselves. It makes your students unified and your team unified, and motivate them to win in the classroom, in life and win ball games.

Self-Awareness- *(What They Think About Themselves)- Action Written Exercises:*

1. Have your students, mentees or athletes write on a sheet of paper their feelings of <u>what they think about themselves</u> negatively and positively. The word "Negative Behavior" should be written on the left side and the word "Positive Behavior" should be written on the right side. Both words should be titled at the top of the page with a vertical line drawn down the center of the paper. They may also number their paper with the amount of negative or positive responses they each may have. After they each complete their list (negative and positive), talk about it and then have them cut the paper in half vertically down the center with scissors, and ball

up the half of the paper with the negative list and throw it in the trash to show that they are no longer following those negative traits, feelings, thoughts, emotions, behaviors, situations and people in their lives.

For the positive list, print out a large heart that is not colored and is almost the size of the 8.5x11 paper, make copies of it, pass the copies out to your students, mentees or athletes and have each of them cut their heart out and add only the positive things from their positive list inside of their heart. Lastly, have them color it. They will use the heart as a new self-awareness heart and vision that they each will practice thinking and believing about themselves every day. It will help with removing negativity and adding positivity about themselves, as this will help make a positive campus and classroom environment for learning for all students, mentees and athletes.

Example of what the paper should look like:

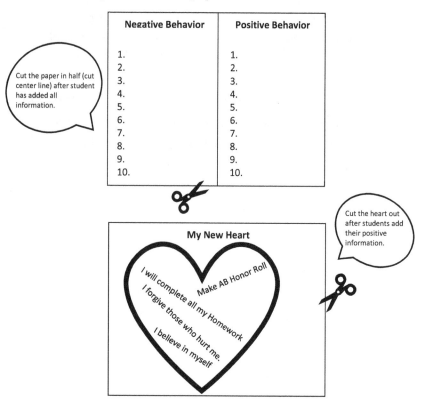

2. Have your students, mentees or athletes develop a social and emotional journal sharing their feelings and emotions of what they each <u>think about themselves</u> no matter what they are. They can share if they want to in a group session.
3. You and your students, mentees or athletes will make a list of short-term and long-term goals and take 5-10 minutes each day and go over them with your students, mentees or athletes to see who have completed their goals. The purpose of this is to teach your students, mentees and athletes that it is important to set goals and gives them short-term motivation and long-term vision to complete them.

It focuses their acquisition of knowledge and helps them to organize their time and their resources, so they can make the most of their life positively and in a gritty way. You may give incentives and rewards to those who complete their goals first. I have learned in my years of experience working with students—elementary, middle school, high school and on the college level that they love it when you reward them for their hard work, and it motivates them to work harder. Please note, you are not using rewards to make them think that it takes rewarding them to make them change or to accomplish their goals. However, you are only showing them that if they work hard and complete their short-term and long-term goals, they can be rewarded. Your rewards are not given every time they complete their goals.

Self-Awareness- *(What They Think About Others)- Action Written Exercises:*

1. Have your students, mentees or athletes write on a sheet of paper their feelings of <u>what they think about others</u> negatively and positively. The word "Negative Behavior" should be written on the left side and the word "Positive Behavior" should be written on the right side. Both words should be titled at the top on of the page with a vertical line drawn down the center of the paper. The students may also number their paper with the amount of negative and positive responses they each may have. After they complete their list (negative and positive), talk about it and then have them cut the paper in half vertically down the center with scissors, and ball up the half of the paper with the negative list and throw it in the trash to show that they are no longer following

those negative traits, feelings, thoughts, emotions, behaviors, situations and people in their lives.

For the positive list, print out a large heart that is not colored and is almost the size of the paper, make copies of it, pass them out to your students, mentees or athletes and have each of them cut their heart out and add only the positive things from their positive list inside of their heart about what they feel about others, and lastly, have them color it. They will use this heart as a new self-awareness heart and vision that they each will practice thinking and believing about others every day. Removing negativity and adding positivity about themselves will help make a positive campus and classroom environment for learning for all students.

The Power of Grit in the Classroom, School, and Community

Example of what the paper should look like:

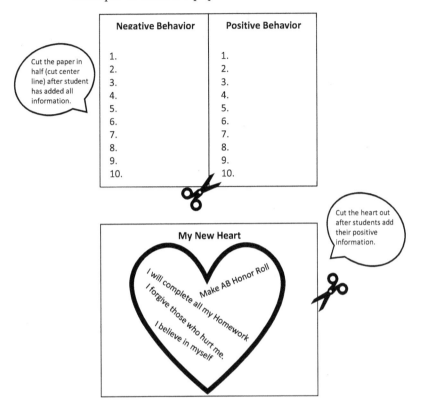

2. Have your students, mentees or athletes develop a social and emotional journal sharing their feelings and emotions of what they <u>think about others</u> no matter what and who they are. They can share if they want to in a group session.
3. Make a list of short-term and long-term work toward goals and take 5-10 minutes each day and go over them with your students or mentees to see who have completed their goals. The purpose of this is to teach your students, mentees and athletes that it is important to set goals and gives them short-term motivation and long-term vision to complete them.

It focuses their acquisition of knowledge and helps them to organize their time and their resources, so that they can make the most of their lives positively and in a gritty way. You may give incentives and rewards to those who have completed their goals. I have learned in my years of experience working with students— elementary, middle school, high school and on the college level that they love it when you reward them for their hard work, and it motivates them to work harder. Please note, you are not using rewards to make them think that it takes rewarding them to make them change or to accomplish their goals. You are only showing them that if they work hard and complete their short-term and long-term goals, they can be rewarded. This is not given every time they complete their goals.

Self-Awareness- *Physical Exercises:*

1. Teach your students, mentees or athletes to pay attention to their approach. Watch how they approach their peers and how they approach situations that do not pertain to them. You can also do this with your colleagues as a teacher or principal collaboration. Their approach should be in a positive way, not over aggressive and way out of line.
2. Build and exercise a pause, plan, and create response habit. This is where your students, mentees or athletes will pause before speaking or reacting to disagreement, conflict or when they are uncomfortable. Plan to react in a paused and planned way and create a habit coming across in a positive way no matter the environment, person or situation. This is a repeated exercise; however, it is a physical exercise that can be done in your classroom, home and/or school.

Get the number of blank sheets of paper you need for the number of students, mentees or athletes you have in your classroom or on your team. Pass them out to them. Have them draw a line down the center of the sheet of paper—divide it into two parts. On the left side of the paper, write a name on their emotions or feelings they feel negatively. Have them list as many names, emotions and feelings that they feel about those persons as they can. On the right side of the sheet of paper, have them write positive things about those persons, emotions, and feelings. It may be hard for some of your students to complete this. However, it is a start to help them express themselves and have positive feelings and emotions toward those persons they have negative feelings or emotions toward, or someone who have hurt them.

3. Have your students to practice the breathing exercise. Teach them to always take a breath when in conflict with another student, teacher, principal parent(s) or their friend(s). Teach them that it is always best to take a breath before acting out or yelling something that they may live to regret.

Self-Awareness- *Reflection Writing*:

The Reflection Writing points below can be given to your students, mentees or athletes as a lesson, class or team exercise, or writing guided practice. I have used these below within my mentoring sessions with my mentees and they have been very effective within our discussions and interventions.

1. Use prompt questions to encourage self-awareness.
2. Name a time when you were the happiest in your life. Why was it the happiest time for you?
3. What is your wildest dream?

4. Name your best friend(s). What do they mean to you? How do you feel when you are around them?
5. Why is it important to be kind to others?
6. Name somethings you like and dislike about yourself?
7. Is it good to hate others who may hate you?
8. Should you dislike someone because they dislike you?
9. Does negative behavior effect making good grades?

Curriculum and Instruction

How Does Curriculum & Instruction Fit into Culture, Leadership, and Learning on Your Campus or Classroom?

This is My Sample: Jane Doe Forest High School
(Not actual school)
School Year: August 30, 2021

Culture	Leadership	Learning
Collaborate to support student learning	Collaborate to support student learning	Our Vision for Learning: student-led/teacher facilitated instruction
Empower teacher leaders	Model effective instructional strategies	Model and support lesson planning based on district curriculum maps (mapped to state standards)
Support and problem solve to meet needs of ALL learners	Facilitate frequent data conversations	Model and support rigorous & relevant learning with high-impact, research-based

		instructional strategies
Growth mindset for ALL	Facilitate curriculum development w/ teacher leaders	Model and support literacy across the curriculum: Reading, writing, speaking and listening, and language
	Provide professional learning opportunities for teachers, administrators and staff	Model and support active student engagement structures
		Model and support data-driven and differentiated learning

Now add your information below based on your campus or classroom curriculum and instruction, and how it fits into Culture, Leadership, and Learning on your campus and/or district.

Add Your School Name: _____

School Year: _____

Building Principal: _____

Curriculum & Instruction Principal: _____

Culture	Leadership	Learning

Stephanie Franklin

Your Instructional Gritty Play Action Book for Your School and/or Classroom

The Instructional Gritty Play Action Book Well-Defined

The Instructional Gritty Play Action Book is an instructional strategy that I have come up with that instructional coaches, PE coaches or sports coaches can use to assist and collaborate in giving teachers choices with strategies they can use to successfully meet their goals for students in their classrooms every day. It can also help the instructional skills specialist, department head, PE coach, or athletic sports coach to teach and collaborate with the teacher so that the teacher feels more confident about implementing the strategies with students in their classroom. Coaches are very assertive and can be very aggressive showing their leadership with discipline when need be and can help the teacher with classroom behavior, student motivation to learn, and get positive feed backs instead of students up out of their seats distracting the classroom instructional time.

This instructional strategy I am using, and teaching others is instructional—play—action as it is important for you and your staff to be team players so that your campus can grow and are successful throughout each school year.

Instruction—students must have instruction in order to be successful in every class and with every assignment and assessment.

Play—Each teacher calls a lesson that he or she wants his or her students to complete. Their goal should be to push the students to success with various lessons, instructional activities and be confident that the lessons will work to the students understanding.

Action—The student must show action by successfully completing the lesson. If no action is shown by the students after the teacher has explained the lesson, 9 times out of 10 they do not understand the lesson and it would be hard for them to be able to see how to complete the lesson successfully. The teacher must show action by teaching the students, rather than putting them down because they may not be successful on the first try. Or teaching the lesson from your desk and watching the students complete it while you sit and watch from your desk.

Each year it takes grit—perseverance and passion to learn as a teacher, coach and as an administrative leader throughout the school year. Also, while working with so many personalities, the academic instructional plays will help teachers to be successful in their classrooms; and administrative leaders be successful throughout their campus.

There are no "I's" in "TEAM." Everyone is important and plays a crucial part in winning the academic instructional gritty game each day you open your classroom door for your students; and each day the campus doors open. It takes everyone working together to win with no one left behind. Too many school campuses are separated and segregated, and as a result, the students nor the staff are winning. Everyone thinks of themselves instead of thinking of the students and why they took the job in the first place. It is always about meeting the needs of students.

The Instructional Gritty Play Action Book will assist the coaches with teachers in setting goals for students by using the classroom or campus instructional gritty play action book. This will identify areas that the teacher needs to obtain in his or her classroom and use data to create an academic play (successful lesson that aligns with their department expectations according to state testing standards) within the campus vision- academic instructional gritty play action book. Coaches, teachers, and principals will all set a goal that will empower your students, and compel the coaches, teachers and administrators to win each day in his or her classroom, along with principals on their campus and the coaches within their PE classes, athletes and sporting arenas.

Instructions for the Academic Instructional Gritty Play Action Book:

The Academic Instructional Gritty Play Action Book make goal setting easier, faster and more effective within each teacher's classroom (Creating a classroom environment that draws the students to want to learn. You will need your own paper to complete the play action book. You will need a budding partner (a coach and another teacher that does not have to be next door to your classroom). The coach will serve as the liaison and the teacher partner will serve as just that—a partner or teammate that will help complete the gritty play action book together and report your results and answers to the coach and to your campus leader and/or appraiser.

Actual Academic Instructional Gritty Play Action Book:

- **Practice-** (You Must Prepare and have a passion to win with students and staff);
- **The Locker Room Experience-** (You Must Persevere and not give up during the game: (teachers- giving the lesson when it appears as if the students are not learning or interested. Students- completing the lesson and may not understand the lesson right away. Administrators- burnt out with students not staying in classes, tardy to class all the time, and roaming the halls during instruction);
- **Half Time-** (Take a break. Take your second wind- You Got This!) Take a second wind and get back in the game and correct those areas that need improvement—either on your campus, within the staff and teachers, and/or within the classroom;
- **Finishing the Game Stronger and Tougher Than Ever-** As I was a successful track runner when I was a little girl on up to 19 years old, I can remember running the 400-yard dash among running many other races. Each time, during the race, as I approached the last 100 yards, I wanted to quit and give

up. But I did not. I took a second wind and finished strong, tougher and gave it all I had until the end. Many times, teachers, staff, assistant principals, building principals, staff and school campus' give up toward the end of the year after all testing has gone forth; and all activities are slowly completing, you can have the tendency to want to quit and become very fatigued, but that is when you have to take a second breath and begin preparing for next year to get better and better within your instructional strategies in your classroom and on school campus. I too have struggled with this area. It is contagious. I'm sure no one is trying to give up or quit, however, it is normal to have these feelings as all you can think about is summer nearing and vacation time is of the essence. But you must take a second wind and finish stronger and tougher than ever no matter what campus you teach or lead on;

- **Practice Again-** (You Must Get Better) You must do your research on the course of study you teach in order to find areas for improvement. As I am an athlete, having multitasked in all sporting areas and arenas, one thing I remembered was "practice makes perfect." This is something that I say and have said to myself, my students, my mentees, and to some of my colleagues. Without practice, your game cannot be perfected or get better. You must practice and you must attend different professional developments, workshops, and virtual online webinars when they are offered as much as you can in order to improve as a teacher, staff, assistant principal, or principal. No one is perfect; however, we should all strive for perfection every day.

There is a reason why I added "Practice Again." You can never get enough of practice. It is important to practice in order to get better and better. I speak about the topic in my book called: "The Locker Room Experience: *For the Struggling Athlete & Coach, & Tips on How to*

Get Recruited in Sports" I wrote and published this book in October 2003. *"The Locker Room Experience"* helps the struggling athlete and coach deal with the struggles of life: relationships, pressure as an athlete and coach, gives tips on how to get recruited, and helps the reader to triumph and win over each of them; and become better athletes and coaches. Although this book is based on sports, athletes, coaching and mentoring, it still applies to grit and how it is important to persevere through all obstacles, even when your teaching career gets hard and it seems as if the students are not learning and their behavior is not getting any better, your classroom management is failing and nothing you've tried seems to be working. You must go deep and dig up the power of grit and push and persevere until you win. Most of all, DO NOT GIVE UP!

There are so many secret areas in teachers, principals, coaches and athletes lives that is hidden for fear of what people may think or for fear of losing their positions. Believe it or not, teachers, principals, coaches and athletes get scared. They have a life outside of the campus arena. Things happen in their own personal lives that are uncontrollable such as, death in their family, a tragic accident, best friend move away, loved ones get sick, failing marriages, struggling co-parenting, child or children get sick, children failing academically and have no will to want to go to school and win with their education. There is so much more to the life of teachers, principals, coaches and athletes, and yet they are still responsible for coming to school and leading and keeping a straight face and showing the gritty attitude so that students can succeed each day. I applaud each of you and encourage you all to keep pushing, persevering and keeping the gritty attitude. I push you to win and not lose.

Following the Academic Instructional Gritty Play Action Book helps the struggling teacher, administrator, coach, athlete and parent to overcome and win the game of life, and instructional game with students each school day.

Stephanie Franklin

Below are three Gritty Play Actions from my Gritty Play Action Book 1-3 I have created. If you are a teacher, see if you can answer the questions by putting yourself in those positions while thinking of your classroom. And if you are a principal, answer the questions by thinking of your position on your campus with the students.

Gritty Play Action 1- 1st Play Called:

1. **Time Management Play-** Name a time when you called a play (lesson) that your students looked at you crazy right after you gave them the instructions to the lesson. After naming the lesson, explain what happened.

_____
_____
_____
_____
_____
_____
_____
_____
_____
_____
_____
_____
_____
_____
_____
_____
_____
_____

Gritty Play Action 2- 2nd Play Called:

2. **Planning Play-** When the ball (the lesson you assigned and liked) was kicked to you, what yard line did you get to

before you were tackled? Were you successful with the lesson you liked after you presented it to your students? Or did you fail? Or were you successful with the lesson that your students needed rather than liked?

___

Gritty Play Action 3- 3rd Play Called:

3. **Learning Environment Play-** When the volleyball *(Assigned activity lesson causing your students to engage with each other to find the answers to questions and/or assignments they do not understand)* was set to you by the setter *(your department chair and skills specialist)*, did you spike it? Or did you miss the spike *(the assigned activity lesson)*, or did you hit it in the net *(was unsuccessful with each student's learning, and understanding the lesson enough to find the answers to the assigned activity and/or assignment)*?

Stephanie Franklin

Questions to Ponder Over:

1. If you could accomplish the goal of the Gritty Action Play Book 1-3, would it really matter? If you could change it, what would you do differently?

2. What teaching strategy can you use to achieve your goal to help your students understand the challenging lessons you assign?

Stephanie Franklin

Create Your Own Academic Instructional <u>Gritty</u> Action Play Book for Your School and/or Classroom Below.

Stephanie Franklin

Strategies for Learner-Friendly Environment Survey

Check your campus and/or classroom environment, place a check on how yours apply below. If your environment is all 4's or 5's, you are in good shape. If your numbers are between 1-3, check with your administrator or appraiser who handles these areas to help you make proper changes.

Order

	1	2	3	4	5
Good lighting (natural, soft, bright just right)					
Comfortable and inviting (temperature, furniture, equipment)					
Everything has its own place and flows					
Expectations/norms/targets posted					

Cleanliness

	1	2	3	4	5
Clutter-free					
Hand sanitizer available					
Smells nice					
Clean floor/carpets					
Clean desks/furniture/computer centers					

Signs of Life

	1	2	3	4	5
Colorful walls/ photos/ posters					
Student's work is displayed					
Student "A- Wall" displays students best "A" work on various assignments					
Is an environment for Learning					
Positive personality of students/teacher reflected					
Plants/ flowers					
Class library					

Layout/Student Accessibility

	1	2	3	4	5
Accessible to move around					
Students can easily access materials, books, supplies					
Easy to do teamwork					
Age-appropriate furniture/materials					

THE GRIT BUCKET LIST

Barriers to Educational Opportunity That Challenges Gritty Achievement

The following families 1-8 are examples of real-life families where students come from. I teach and mentor these types of students every school day. After reviewing the families below, you as a teacher or administrator can identify with these types of student's families as these types of students show up in your classrooms and schools each school day. The students I teach and mentor, are majority at-risk students challenged with mobility rates that has to do with homelessness, foster placements, neglect, living in project apartments, low-income status, and low rated living conditions. There are barriers in every student's family that causes them to not learn at their highest academic level and achievement. Usually, these students are picked by society to likely fail their classes and dropping out is at the highest rate instead of high school graduation.

Barriers causes these types of students to be disengaged from school. They are from low socioeconomic status families and homes where the parents were high school dropouts. I have had students mention that earlier schooling did not prepare them for high school, which is the reason for their poor performance and lack of educational interest.

As grit relates to persevering and setting a goal to reach long-term goals at all costs, this is opposite of what we see in our school systems as most students are less persistent and persevering. They are disengaged and are not successful in their classes and studies. Teachers are having to work harder to teach and deal with misbehaving students with these types of attitudes. As a teacher and mentor on my campus and sponsoring and leading an afterschool mentor program at my school campus, it is a challenge each school day to make sure my students and mentees have a gritty drive to win no matter what challenges they may face at school, at home and in their community. I teach them grit—to have passion and perseverance to set short-term and long-term goals until they reach them. I teach them to be persistent even when they face obstacles that make them want to quit or to drop out and turn to the streets. I teach my students and mentees to stick with whatever they start and endure until the task they started is completed. I teach them to work hard even after experiencing hardship, academic difficulty and failure. Families 1-8, on my chart, shows the type of students I teach and mentor each school day.

As teachers, staff, leaders, coaches, and administrators, you are responsible for understanding every student that walk through your classroom door—where they each come from, help build culture among them and push them to win through every gritty obstacle to achievement.

After reviewing my chart below, add the barriers in your classroom and/or school on the chart below my chart and write your own *Barriers to Educational Opportunity That Challenges Gritty Achievement* chart as they relate to the students you teach each school day. Afterwards write areas for improvement where you can reach your students better with these types of challenges, build culture, and raise a positive socioeconomic rate in your classroom and/or school.

Family #1	Family #2	Family #3	Family #4
• Family of 4 • Mother & 3 children • Caucasian • English speaking • High school dropout	• Family of 3 • Father, Mother, & 1 son • Father & Mother are Latino • Bilingual	• Family of 5 • Mother, daughter, two sons, & grandson	• Family of 3 • Two mothers, & 1 daughter

• Homeless, live with friends, grandmother, or in a shelter with no transportation.	• Mother and father are college educated with no degrees. Mother and father are both professionals	• Family is African American • English speaking • Parents have high school education but no diplomas • Live from paycheck to paycheck. • No savings; car was recently stolen	• Mothers are Caucasian • Both mothers are college educated professionals
Family #5	**Family #6**	**Family #7**	**Family #8**
• Family of 2 • Daughter & mother • Caucasian • English speaking • Prior drug use and has resulted in loss of jobs Live in a minivan	• Family of 7 • Father, mother, & 5 children • Spanish speaking • Parents and 4 of the children are undocumented Parents are illiterate	• Family of 4 • Mother, father, & 2 children • Bilingual • Asian-American Father is a fisher; Mother is a grocery clerk	• Family of 5 • Mother, father, & 3 children • Native Americans • Bilingual Parents are college educated professionals

Write the Barriers to Educational Opportunity That Challenges Gritty Achievement in <u>Your</u> Classroom

Family #1	Family #2	Family #3	Family #4

Family #5	Family #6	Family #7	Family #8

After you have filled in your answers from the Barriers to Educational Opportunity That Challenges Gritty Achievement chart from the previous pages, answer the following questions below:

1. What families did you find to be the worst of all families with challenges? Why?

___

2. Did the one(s) you chose remind you of any students you have in your class? If so, name one or some. You may also talk about it or share it in your staff meeting, department meeting, or among a colleague.

3. What do you plan to incorporate within your lessons and classroom from your personal chart to better these types of barriers you see in your students? Remember your goal should be to raise the level of grit within your students and set an atmosphere that challenges them to learn against all odds. Please be specific.

_____
_____
_____
_____
_____
_____
_____
_____
_____
_____
_____
_____
_____
_____
_____
_____
_____
_____
_____
_____
_____
_____
_____
_____
_____
_____
_____

Index

1. "gritty famous people." — Google, pg. 55.
2. Introduction- "Is the Jar full or half full?," LU University (2020). pg. 13.
3. Angela Duckworth (2016), pg. 27.
4. Cook (2020) Teaching Grit. Google, pg. 39.
5. TpT Pins (2020), pg. 288.
6. PBIS- Stands for Positive Behavior Interventions Systems. It is a three-tiered, research -based framework designed by each school, containing fundamental elements for increasing positive behavior and decreasing negative behavior. It establishes a social culture, and the behavior supports needed to improve social, emotional, behavioral, and academic outcomes for all students (Google, 2020). pg. 69.
7. Dweck (2015)
8. Peterson (2015), pg. 77.
9. Golden (2017), pg. 77.
10. Grit Poster Samples, Google, pg. 55.
11. Angela Duckworth, (2016), pg. 27.
12. Google- RTI (Response to Intervention), pg. 19.
13. Google- ELL/ESL/TESOL, pg. 19.
14. Google- Domains 1-4, pg. 29.
15. Google- Social-Emotional Learning (SEL), pg. 97, 222.
16. Google- Collaborative for Academic, Social, and Emotional Learning (CASEL), pg. 98.
17. Google- *https://www.sacap.edu.za/blog/applied-psychology/what-is-grit/*
18. *Social and Emotional Learning: Why Students Need It. What Districts are Doing About It.*

Index

19. *T-TESS- Texas Teacher Evaluation & Support System (Appraiser Handbook), pg.219.*
20. *Lamar University- Beaumont,* Recruitment and On-Board Actions. *https://www.lamar.edu/career-and-testing-services/employers1.html*
21. Collaborative for Academic, Social, and Emotional Learning (CASEL) (Google, 2021), *pg. 98.*
22. Instructional Gritty Play Action Book, 267.
23. David Zerfoss, *The Empty Pickle Jar,* (Google, 2011) Introduction. pg. 13.
24. *Stress Is a Choice,* by Dave Zerfoss, (2011), pg. 13, 115.
25. Lindsey, D. B., & Lindsey, R. B. (2016). *Build cultural proficiency to ensure equity.* Journal of Staff Development.
26. Every kid needs a champion | Rita Pierson, *http://www.youtube.com/watch?v=SFnMTHhKdkw*
27. Sparks, Sarah. *Study: RTI Practice Falls Short of Promise.* (Education Week, (2015)). pg. 120.
28. "Where there is a will, there is a way" should be reversed and restated as "Where there is a way, there is a will." –Jean Anyon, Radical Possibilities, 2005.
29. Social Emotional Learning- WHY SEL? https://www.youtube.com/watch?v=Pq_wd-jQNEg
30. The Maslow's hierarchy of needs that categories needs as "existence needs, desires for satisfying interpersonal relationships; and growth needs, desires for continued personal growth and development" (Ehiobuche, 2013). pg. 126.
31. (Google, 2021)- Growth Mindset believes that ability can change as a result of effort, perseverance, and practice. You may hear a student say, "Math is hard, but if I keep trying and studying, I can get better at it." Students will growth mindsets see mistakes as ways to learn, embrace challenges, and persist in the face of setbacks. pg. 55.

32. (Google, 2021)- Fixed Mindset is where students believe their basic abilities, their intelligence, their talents, are just fixed traits. Whereas with growth mindsets students understand that their talents and abilities can be developed through effort, good teaching, persistence. pg. 55.
33. "Let's get in good trouble, necessary trouble…" —John Lewis (Google 2021).
34. Google, 2021) ERG theory. It is the development of Maslow's hierarchy of needs that categories needs as, "existence needs, desires for satisfying interpersonal relationships; and growth needs, desires for continued personal growth and development" (Ehiobuche, 2013). pg. 122.
35. Grit stands for building and developing culture and emphasizing character (Deanyy, 2014). pg. 123.
    -Developing Grit in Our Students: *Why Grit is Such a Desirable Trait, and Practical Strategies for Teachers and Schools.* By Jennifer Bashant, Ph.D.
    https://files.eric.ed.gov/fulltext/EJ1081394.pdf
33. Houston Food Bank, pg. 127, 150.
    https://www.houstonfoodbank.org/find-help/agency-locator/?gclid=EAIaIQobChMIjZOv9ObN8AIVhPfjBx32uwnzEAAYAiAAEgJKoPD_BwE
34. Think-Pair-Share- also allows students wait time (McTighe & Lyman, 1988). pg. 232, 239.
35. Turn to Your Neighbor, https://tiee.esa.org/teach/tutorials/neighbor.html. pg. 232, 239.
36. Jigsaw Classroom- The jigsaw classroom is a research-based cooperative learning technique invented and developed in the early 1970s by Elliot Aronson and his students at the University of Texas and the University of California. https://www.jigsaw.org/#:~:text=OVERVIEW-

Index

,OVERVIEW,and%20the%20University%20of%20California. pg. 10, 233.
37. Value Line- https://www.learningforjustice.org/classroom-resources/teaching-strategies/community-inquiry/value-lines. pg. 10, 235, 240.
38. Round Table- Model Teaching: *Better Education for Better Educators*. 2021. https://www.modelteaching.com/education-articles/teaching-strategies/re-energizing-classroom-discussion-through-round-table-circles, pg. 10, 235, 236, 241.
39. Checklist: *Cooperative Learning Success Factors,* https://resources.corwin.com/sites/default/files/Checklist_Cooperative_Learning.pdf. pg. 238.
40. (Google-2021)- Response to Intervention (RTI) is a multi-tier approach to the early identification and support of students with learning and behavior needs. pg. 118, 198.
41. PBIS- Stands for Positive Behavior Interventions Systems. It is a three-tiered, research -based framework designed by each school, containing fundamental elements for increasing positive behavior and decreasing negative behavior. It establishes a social culture, and the behavior supports needed to improve social, emotional, behavioral, and academic outcomes for all students (Google- 2021). pg. 69, 288.
42. Grit stands for building and developing culture and emphasizing character (Dean, 2014). pg. 145.
43. "Interventions are building relationships, adapting the environment, managing sensory stimulation, changing communication strategies, providing prompts and clues, using a teach, review, and reteach process, and developing social skills" (Google, 2021) pg. 199.
44. Read Out Loud and the Wordless Treatment. What this means is the reading teacher will read out loud to their students as the students follow along using the wordless

treatment, meaning no words at all. They all are totally quiet—they will not comment or ask questions pertaining to what the teacher is reading to them. (Google, 2021) pg. 200.

45. Echo Reading- What this means is the students will repeat what the teacher has read for understanding and clarity. (Google, 2021) pg. 201.
46. Paired Reading- What this means is the teacher will pair two students with each other and have them read to each other aloud for understanding and clarity. (Google, 2021) pg. 201.
47. Listening Performance- What this means is the teacher will watch each student closely to make sure they understood. (Google, 2021) pg. 201.
48. Repeated Reading- What this means is the teacher will make the students repeat what the teacher read for understanding and clarity. (Google, 2021) pg. 201.
49. **T-**TESS Appraisal, https://teachfortexas.org/Views/Appraiser, pg. 208.
50. *Whipple, Percy Edwin. Grit is the grain that builds character. https://www.passiton.com/inspirational-quotes/8274-grit-is-the-grain-of-character, pg. 4.*
51. *Smith, Paul Bradley. Grit is the persistence in following your own destiny. https://www.quoteslyfe.com/quote/Grit-is-the-persistence-in-following-your-22753, pg. 204.*
52. *Hall, Jerry. Grit is having the courage to do the right thing, regardless of the popularity or consequences. https://bayart.org/mediocrity-quotes/. pg. 4.*
53. *H. Diamonds, Peter. What is grit? Grit is refusing to give up. It's persistence. https://quotebanner.com/quotes/peter-diamandis-quote-49255/what-is-grit-grit-is-refusing-to-give-up-its-persistence-its-making-your-own-luck. pg. 4.*
54. *Lewis, Sarah. "Grit is not just simple elbow-grease term for rugged persistence. It is an often-invisible display of endurance that lets you stay in an uncomfortable place, work hard to improve upon a given interest and do it again and again." https://www.culturalfront.org/2015/12/the-rise-grit-of-arts-pt-2.html, pg. 4.*

Chapter 22, Is Grit a Character Trait?
Professional Development 3
Answer KEY

Question	Add Your Answer
4. Name the 4 Dimensions listed in the T-TESS Rubric.	1. Planning 2. Instruction 3. Learning Environment 4. Professional Practices and Responsibilities
8. On the T-TESS Rubric, what does the "LEARNING ENVIRONMENT DIMENSION 3.2 Managing Student Behavior" establishes?	The teacher establishes, communicates and maintains clear expectations for student behavior.
9. What are the Appraisal Guidelines (T-TESS) and what role do they play?	The appraiser has a vital role in assessing teaching proficiency and ensuring that teachers and administrators derive reliable and meaningful information from the teacher evaluation process... appraisers help teachers and administrators make decisions that support efforts to improve instructional quality and student performance. https://teachfortexas.org/Views/Appraiser

Professional Development #3, Session 2 Scavenger Hunt

Table 1- Clue Card 1

Answer to the Scavenger Hunt-

What is social behavior of students?

Social behavior is defined as including social skills deficits, behavior under inadequate stimulus control, and inappropriate behavior in the classroom.

Meet the Author

Stephanie Franklin,

M.Th., M.DIV., M.Ed., D. Ed. *Candidate* has been writing for years and love it. She has exemplified excellence through her education with 3 master's degrees—Theological Studies, Divinity, Education Administration and is a doctorate candidate with an emphasis in Educational Leadership. She has also taught on a college level. She is a worldwide published author, educator, mentor, entrepreneur and more. She is doing it again with *"The Power of Grit in the Classroom, School and Community."* She has found with writing this book, those who are successful are not successful by avoiding making mistakes, however, they are successful by continuing to persevere after making mistakes to reach their goals—grit is the result.

If you would like to contact Stephanie:
info@stephaniefranklin.org

Places to purchase her book worldwide:
Amazon, Barnes & Noble, Books-A-Million, Borders, Walmart, and anywhere books are sold.